THE SUCCESS OF SMALL GROUPS AS A DISCIPLESHIP MODEL IN THE 21ST CENTURY CHURCH

L. LAWRENCE BRANDON, D.Min.

BK Royston Publishing
Jeffersonville IN
http://bkroystonpublishing.com
bkroystonpublishing@gmail.com

© 2024

All Rights Reserved. No part of this book may be reproduced, stored in a retrieval system, or transmitted by any means without the written permission of the author.

Cover and Layout: BK Royston Publishing

Good News Translation (GNT) - (Today's English Version, Second Edition) © 1992 American Bible Society. All rights reserved. For more information about GNT, visit www.bibles.com and www.gnt.bible.

King James Version (KJV) — Public Domain

New International Version (NIV) - Holy Bible, New International Version®, NIV® Copyright ©1973,

ISBN-13: 978-1-967282-23-4
Hardback ISBN: 978-1-967282-24-1

Printed in the United States of America

Dedication

This project is wholeheartedly dedicated to my beloved momma, the late Mother Helen B. Lyons, and the late Dr. Oral Roberts, who have been the sources of inspiration, and who gave me strength when I thought of giving up. It is also dedicated to my wife, Wanda L. Brandon, my children, and my Praise Temple family who continually provided their moral, spiritual, emotional, and financial support. This project is also dedicated to Dr. James Barber, Ms. Celine Butler, and Mrs. Melanie Tollett who shared their words of advice and encouragement to finish this study.

Finally, I dedicate this work to the Almighty God, Jesus: thank you for the guidance, strength, power of mind, protection, and skills, as well as for giving me a healthy life. LORD, for this I rededicate my life to and for you.

Acknowledgements

Thanks are extended to my supervisor, Dr. Robert Griffin, for providing guidance and feedback throughout this project. Thanks also go to my wife, Wanda, and to the staff and members of Praise Temple of Shreveport, Louisiana, and of Evergreen Missionary Baptist Church of Oakland, California, for putting up with me sitting in the office for hours on end, and for providing guidance and a sounding board when required. I particularly thank my children, Jasmine Nicole, Isaiah Jerel, Elijah Terel, and Queenesia Beatrice, for their patience and encouragement. Thanks go to my eldest son, the late Larry Lawrence Brandon, III: I sorely miss you.

Table of Contents

Dedication	iii
Acknowledgements	iv
What is Discipleship?	1
Discipleship Ministry Opportunity	5
Discipleship Setting for Our Study	7
Definitions of Terms	16
Modern Status of Discipleship: A Reflection	21
Biblical Perspective	24
The Concept of Biblical Fellowship	27
Historical-Theological	31
Cultural and Personal Perspective	44
Small Group and Ministry Models	65
Ministry Models	72
Most Notable Small Group Model	121
The 40-Day Campaign Strategy	130
The Mid-Sized Geographic Strategy	131
Cell-Based Church	132
Missional Communities	133
Small Group Research Strategy	133
Rationale for Methodology	138
Nature of the Research Design for the Study	139
Participants	140

Circumstances for Research	143
Research Questions	145
Procedures	146
Analysis	153
Participant Demographics	155
Description of the Research Survey	156
Measures	158
Discipleship research survey	159
Results of the Discipleship Research	161
Participants' Profiles Results	161
Survey Instrument	181
Survey Instrument Results	185
Summary of Results	236
Project Conclusion	240
Systems for Leadership Development	243
Integrated Ecosystems for Discipleship	244
Propagating Fertile Discipleship Ecosystems	245
BIBLIOGRAPHY	247
LIST OF TABLES	259
Author Biography	261

What is Discipleship?

Discipleship, in the truest sense, is the act of developing the life of an individual in conjunction with his or her faith walk. Recognizing the importance of connectivity within this measure of relationship, the primary responsibility is to provide a consistent measure of support that includes both guidance and a community that is willing to share. Throughout the Bible, discipleship is reflected and reinforced through the importance of relationship. As people mature and navigate through life, the direct interaction through the sharing of practical expertise yields positive outcomes for those who are becoming disciples.

Discipleship is an active strategy that proves to be an essential focus in any ministry. It is a requirement for successful church growth, as well as spiritual maturity within the life of a person. People come to ministries from various walks of life, and they have a complex list of issues associated with their current lifestyles. In addition to these matters, there are problems that people encounter and have difficulty navigating through by themselves. Discipleship provides direct mentorship through teaching, guidance through experience, support in development, and accountability through attentive action.[1]

Because people are connected across the globe in faith communities, discipleship forges the bonds of communal fellowship and extends person-to-person relationships that open up the way for people to share on a more personal level. With the advancement of the 21st century church and the immeasurable growth of local congregations, the church has become a vivacious environment in which collaborative and inspiring undertakings happen. Ministry models consist of many structures. However, the small group component is the one most frequently used to access people in an intimate

---

[1] Keith R. Anderson and Randy D. Reese, *Spiritual Mentoring: A Guide for Seeking and Giving Direction* (Downers Grove, IL: InterVarsity Press, 1999), 33-34.

setting simultaneously while sharing ideas that give all participants the chance to develop resolutions to real-life issues that they face as members of the faith community.[2] Through the use of small groups, resources have come to provide commendation in regard to the reach of congregational care. The use of small groups has expanded the extent of ministry resources that are not only available, but are readily obtainable at any time. Additionally, using small groups has decreased specific needs related to membership neglect, awareness of congregational needs, and lack of accountability, which have limited effective ministry models in the past. The use of the extension that is referred to as small groups has provided to both church and member the capabilities to engage each other as well as interrelate. Small

---

[2] Send Institute, "Church Planting Manifesto," *Sendinstitute.org*, n.d., p. 2, https://www.sendinstitute.org/wp-content/uploads/2019/02/2.7-Draft-Send-Institute- Church-Planting-Manifesto-for-North-America.pdf (11 December 2020).

groups advance a diverse slate of adapted support structures for members to engage in communal faith-growing experiences.

Small groups have provided the necessary connections for collaboration among a variety of ministry approaches in order to engage congregants on every level while strengthening the impact of local ministry.[3] They have also proven themselves to be aa essential influence in providing a foundation for extensive congregational care through constantly making updated and expanded resources available to improve the lives of a ministry's membership. Although the use of small groups is a collaborative strategy used within discipleship, it is intended principally to dispense support to members while offering an opportunity for them to interact through the auspices of fellowship.

---

[3] In Ho Jei, "A Strategy on Small Group Leadership Development for Transitioning of Gaeumjung Church into a Cell-Based Church" (D.Min. proj., Liberty Theological Seminary, 2008), 12-13.

Discipleship Ministry Opportunity

Small groups, even in the midst of the expansive changes that they have brought to the modern-era church structure, have created many methodical disputes and pressurized circumstances, such as apprehension, dissatisfaction, strain, and stress for church leadership in an attempt to meet congregational needs while remaining as tangible fixtures in church life.[4] Therefore, many ministry leaders have become cautious, opposing and discounting of the use of small groups in their discipleship models and congregational care practices. This project will examine potential influences that provide an explanation for the differences and perspectives in how ministries make use of the small-group platform in their local church settings. The circumstances surrounding small groups have caused discontent, which has led to stress for ministry leaders in their attempt to accommodate the ever-expanding

---

[4] Thomas G. Kirkpatrick, Small Groups in the Church: A Handbook for Creating Community (New York: Alban Institute, 1995), 100.

needs of growing congregations while managing a stable ministry dynamic. Therefore, many ministry leaders have become careful, divergent, and disregarding of the practice of small groups in their discipleship paradigms and their congregational care preparations.

This project will submit evidence to provide clarification for the changes and viewpoints regarding how ministries utilize the small group program in their local church settings.

Current research has shown that churches regard the small group model as a component for educational and personal benefits to the connectivity within their congregations; nevertheless, very few churches fully merge the small group into every aspect of church activity. Furthermore, it seems that previous research in this area has failed to examine the exclusive limitations that are confronted by individual discipleship models, as well as the specific attitudes that are developed, as a result of using the small group in the church of today.

Discipleship Setting for Our Study

There will be 200 small group participants who currently live in metropolitan Shreveport, Louisiana. Small group participants will range in age from 20 to 65 years. The sample of participants will be solicited only from the Consolidated Metropolitan Full Gospel Baptist Church (CMFGBC). The participants will vary from general members to outsiders who fellowship within the small group ministry setting. This ministry entity is a Full Gospel Baptist Church that was established in the doctrinal teaching of Pentecostalism and Charismatic Christianity. Additionally, there has been redevelopment in the programming and ministry design within the past ten years. The research site has been assigned an acronym. This acronym represents the actual church; thus, the acronym is used to protect the privacy of the institutions (per the policy agreed upon when receiving approval to conduct the study).

CMFGBC was founded in the spring of 1992. On March 24, 1992, the bishop and six members met to organize CMFGBC. The church began, originally, with prayer service and Bible study in the home of a deacon and deaconess in Bossier City, Louisiana. In this modest beginning, the church committed to the great commission of the Lord to evangelize and win the lost at all costs. In April of 1992, the church was incorporated as a non-profit organization. On Sunday, April 19, 1992, the church held its first worship service in Shreveport, Louisiana. The membership immediately grew from seven to thirty. The church remained at that location until September, 1992, when it moved. During the second year of existence, CMFGBC became known as the "Church where the doors swing on the hinges of love." CMFGBC also coined the phrases "Spiritual Hospital" and "House of Refuge" due to the heightened care and concern for God's people. In September of 1993, the growth of CMFGBC accelerated beyond its capacity.

In October of 1993, the church moved to a storefront. Once

again, growth accelerated tremendously to approximately 200 members. On Easter Sunday, 1996, CMFGBC formed a motorcade and entered its current location in Shreveport, Louisiana. The church's dedication to Bishop Paul S. Morton and the Full Gospel Baptist Church Fellowship was so great that in May, 1997, the name of the church was officially changed to CMFGBC. On Easter Sunday, 1997, CMFGBC expanded their current ministry and branched out, thereby making them known as "one church in two cities." CMFGBC currently has more than 900 members on record, including ten spiritual sons and daughters who are pastoring. CMFGBC is currently associated with the Full Gospel Baptist Church Fellowship. The ministry is affiliated with the Home Mission Board of the Southern Baptist Convention and the American Baptist Churches of USA. CMFGBC is also affiliated with the Unity Celebration Fellowship.

The ministry centers its philosophy in creating environments that promote the development of fellowship through intentional practices of growth reflected through communal learning. The participants within this study will consist of all participants of the small (cell) groups at CMFGBC. The participants will be recruited on the grounds that they are active small (cell) group members. Additionally, they will be recruited because there has been a recent period when considerable efforts were made towards small group development.

The small group model will be established to enrich the discipleship process of recent members who have connected themselves to the church community. Through this project, the significant impact of employing small (cell) groups hopes to be seen in a designated small group that will take place on a weekly basis. The groups will consist of 200 participants. Small groups are localized discipleship environments, and documentation shows the essential nature of their presence within the church through the expanding of congregational care practices in ministry. The project will establish an understanding of the necessity and effectiveness of small groups in developing an effective model of discipleship in the 21st century church.

The small groups will be formed as a test model to improve the individual care and concern for the congregation and community. Additionally, the small group model will be utilized to enhance the discipleship of newly-joined members in the church community. The scheduled meetings of the small groups will take place on Tuesday evenings at 6:30 p.m. The groups will consist of 200 participants. The small groups will undertake a slate of studies on such topics as contemporary issues, books of the Bible, or sermon-based materials. All materials related to the groups will be purchased by the local congregation.

The design of this analysis will be intentionally pursued to investigate the hypotheses of this project and to survey cause-and-effect, while making related subsequent projections. The participants will be a convenience sample selected to study the specified variables. The quantitative data that are particular to this specific design will be based on precise measurements using structured and validated data-collection instruments. The evaluation research will be conducted through data collection from the small groups, beginning during the first session when group participants will be asked to complete a survey. Over a period of three to six months, participants will be asked to provide feedback regarding their growth during their time of participation with the small groups. The identification of statistical relationships will be essential, while objectivity will remain critical. The researcher's biases will not be known to the participants within the study. The participant characteristics will be deliberately concealed from the researcher. The research inquiry will produce findings that are generalizable to other populations.

The rationale behind this study's quantitative focus is to determine the effectiveness and progression of the use of small groups to create an effective model of discipleship in the 21st

century church. The study will give pastors and ministry leaders a new perspective on how to propel small group offerings and fellowship experiences to a completely new height with endless potential. The small group is a type of high-impact practice in ministry settings. According to Carl F. George, "The small group proposal represents a long-term solution as well: If implemented properly, not only does the cell method build enduring organizational renewal into itself, but it is never to be repented of."[5] High-impact practices (HIPs) are defined as "active learning practices that promote deep learning by promoting student engagement as measured by the National Survey on Student Engagement (NSSE). To be a high-impact practice, the experience must satisfy the definition established by George Kuh (2008, Kuh & O'Donnell, 2013) and his colleagues . . . ."[6] HIPs are the

---

[5] Carl F. George, Prepare Your Church for the Future (Grand Rapids, MI: Fleming H. Revell, 1992), 71.
[6] University of Wisconsin Eau Claire, "High-Impact Practices," Uwec.edu, n.d., n.p., https://www.uwec.edu/acadaff/academic-master-plan/high-

research-proven top 10 instructional procedures that are the most useful to people of all backgrounds, and are capable of shaping or motivating someone or something in a formidable way. These practices are characterized by their intricate methods and validity in the ministry practice. HIPs can be expanded further through created ministry goals, standards, and intentions. Additionally, HIPs provide a measure for assessing the individuals who participate, as well as the nature of member perception.[7] The goal is to construct the research in such a way that it defines, clarifies, and projects.

The project will provide a distinct perspective from a narrow-angle lens, and would allow the opportunity to test specific hypotheses. The structure of this project will allow the review

---

impact-practices/#:~: text=High%2Dimpact%20practices%2C%20or%20HIPs,on%20Student%20Engagement%20(NSSE) (30 April 2021).

[7] George D. Kuh and Ken O'Donnell, *Ensuring Quality and Taking High-Impact Practices to Scale* (Washington, DC: AAC&U, 2013).

of behaviors under controlled conditions, and will isolate causal effects. Considering these factors, the nature of reality will be that of a single reality combined with the concentration of objectivity. The statistical report will be presented with connections, with comparisons of averages, and with statistical significance of outcomes.

Definitions of Terms

For the purpose of this study, some associated terms are defined in order to provide a clear picture of many facets related to the relationships among technology, pedagogical practices, and teacher experiences.

"Assimilation" is a small modification or movement made to achieve a preferred fit, form, or result. Assimilation occurs when new information is changed to fit into one's schemas (what one already knows). It keeps the new information or experience and adds it to what already exists in one's mind.[8]

"Behavior" is the tendency to adjust to the environment, to familiarize or become comfortable with a new atmosphere; adapt.[9]

"Church growth" is "growth in the number of baptized

---

[8] W. Huitt and J. Hummel, "Piaget's Theory of Cognitive Development," *Edpsycinteractive.org*, 2003, n.p., http://www.edpsycinteractive.org/topics/cognition/piaget.html (5 February 2021).

[9] Huitt and Hummel, n.p.

believers and growth in the number of worshipping groups."[10]

"Congregational care" includes "a wide range of ministries and teams, such as visitation with members who are homebound, hospitalized, and in rehabilitation or care facilities, prayer ministry, and hospitality associated with funerals and memorial services."[11]

"Differentiated instruction" is "an effective strategy which many experts recommend for teachers. It is student-aware teaching which recognizes and teaches according to learner differences."[12]

---

[10] John Seamands, "What McGavran's Church Growth Thesis Means," *Missionexus.org*, 1 October 1966, n.p., https://missionexus.org/what-mcgavrans-church-growth-thesis-means/ (5 February 2021).

[11] Martha Lundgren, "A Plan for Congregational and Pastoral Care Giving with Our Senior and Elder Members," *Umcstmarks.org*, April 2016, 3, https://pdf4pro.com/amp/view/a-plan-for-congregational-and-pastoral-care-giving-238a72.html (5 February 2021).

[12] Mariyam Shareefa, Rohani Hj Awg Mat Zin, Nor Zaiham Midawati Abdullah, and Rosmawijah Jawawi, "Differentiated Instruction: Definition and Challenging

"Discipleship" is the process of "becoming more Christ-like," and is used "to describe *the process of spiritual growth*."[13]

"High Impact Practices" (HIP) are those that include the following eight elements:

Performance expectations set at appropriately high levels. . . . Significant investment of time and effort by students over an extended period of time. . . . Interactions with [staff] and peers about substantive matters. . . . Experiences with diversity, wherein students are exposed to and must contend with people and circumstances that differ from those with which students are familiar. . . .
Frequent, timely, and constructive feedback. . . . Periodic, structured opportunities to reflect and integrate learning. . . . Opportunities to discover relevance of learning through real-world applications. . . . Public demonstration of competence.[14]

Factors Perceived by Teachers," *Proceedings of the 3rd International Conference on Special Education (ICSE 2019)* 388 (2019): 322, https://www.atlantis-press.com/proceedings/icse-19/125928885 (5 February 2021).

[13] The Navigators, *The State of Discipleship* (Ventura, CA: Barna Group, 2015), 19.

[14] George D. Kuh and Ken O'Donnell, "Figure 2: High-Impact Practices: Eight Key Elements and Examples," *Ts3.nashonline.org*, 2013, n.p., http://ts3.nashonline.org/wp-content/uploads/2018/04/AACU-LEAP-High-Impact-Practice-Characteristics.pdf (5 February 2021).

"Mentoring," traditionally, "has been defined as a relationship between an older, more experienced mentor and a younger, less experienced protégé for the purpose of helping and developing the protégé's career."[15]

"Religious Communities" are "informal and diverse forms of gatherings for religious purposes such as faith-based organizations, para-church/congregation organizations, campus ministries, and faith-based singles' groups."[16]

"Retention" is an effort by an institution or organization to keep individuals "as an institutional measure."[17]

---

[15] Belle Rose Ragins and Kathy E. Kram, "The Roots and Meaning of Mentoring," in *The Handbook of Mentoring at Work: Theory, Research and Practice*, eds. Belle Rose Ragins and Kathy E. Kram (Los Angeles: Sage Publications, 2007), 5.

[16] William B. Whitney and Pamela Ebstyne King, "Religious Congregations and Communities," in *Emerging Adults' Religiousness and Spirituality: Meaning-Making in an Age of Transition*, ed. Carolyn McNamara Barry and Mona M. Abo-Zena (New York: Oxford University Press, 2014), 134.

[17] Linda Serra Hagedorn, "How to Define Retention: A

"Small Group" is a gathering of "3 to 15 people who meet regularly (weekly, biweekly, or monthly) to help one another grow in holiness of heart and life and to help the congregation participate in God's mission in the world."[18]

New Look at an Old Problem," *Eric.ed.gov*, 2006, 6, https://files.eric.ed.gov/fulltext/ED493674.pdf (5 February 2021).

[18] Steven W. Manskar, *Small-Group Ministries: Christian Formation through Mutual Accountability* (Nashville: Cokesbury, 2012), 6-7.

MODERN STATUS OF DISCIPLESHIP: A REFLECTION

In present-day American society, people live in an increasingly expanding and intersecting world. The culture of modern-day ministry requires that ministry leaders promote an advancing movement towards speaking to all forms of diversity, including physical norms, cultural dynamics, and intellectual foundations that are present throughout diverse ministry settings. The leader's responsibility is to implement structures and programming simultaneously so that members are engaged within the local church environment that is fueled by inclusivity. There is a substantial amount of statistical and factual information that has been developed from previously-conducted studies that describe in detail the progression and transformation of small groups across a visible timeline, as well as their uses in regard to congregational development.

Small groups and their integration into the ministerial practices of the 21st century church have been the center of much dialogue and debate. The integration of various small group types into the discipleship environment has become a critical issue at the center of America's religious agenda. Small groups have become a staple necessity in the acquisition of concepts in the midst of the local church environment. The newest advancements in ministry design have extended the opportunity to the leader and the participant to make use of the benefits of these groups, from small interactions to interconnected fellowships. Even though small groups are utilized as an additional measure for discipleship and instruction, ministry leaders find themselves in an uncomfortable position in regard to incorporating these mechanisms into their current ministry models. However, if properly integrated within any church dynamic, there is visible evidence of the benefits that small groups provide to the creation of a collaborative and interactive learning environment where growth can be experienced.

There are many barriers to integrating small groups into

present-day churches.

The nature of external barriers, such as lack of resources, institution, subject culture, and assessment, are critical areas that will be examined through the literature. On the other end of the spectrum, there are barriers of an intrinsic nature. These particular barriers are specifically unique to the local church and include beliefs, attitudes, and knowledge.

Biblical Perspective

Relationship Rooted in Fellowship

A theology of small groups begins with the character of God. The first small group conceptually occurred in eternity: God the Trinity subsisted as three in one. This can be viewed as a small group. Two of the most imperative statements about God are that God is one (Isa 44:6), and that God's oneness is expressed in three persons—Father, Son, and Spirit (Acts 7:55).[19] This basic affirmation of the Godhead being three in one supports the initial conviction of sincere Christianity. Although God is one and each member of the Trinity is participating in every phase of God's design in creation, it is acceptable to accentuate that the Father was principally at work in crafting people, the Son was specifically at labor in liberating people, and the Spirit is chiefly at work in purifying

---

[19] Unless otherwise indicated, all Bible references in this MRP are to the New American Standard Bible Updated (NASB95) (LaHabra, CA: Lockman Foundation, 1995).

people.

God, although spirit, has been conceptualized as a relational being. People are made in his image (Gen 1:26). Believers are summoned to develop, maintain, and share the bonds of fellowship with all who are part of their faith communities. They are called to do so beyond their relationship with God, and they are to extend themselves to the diversity of creation. People's relationship with their fellow humans is the core of their existence to discover more about God through the experiences of his creations.[20] The Creator has designed the creation to be interconnected in a way that reflects the intended purpose and design for all of humanity.

Relationships are the centralized connecting points in which people find the meaning of human existence. Their interactions are reflected in their engagement of both God and

---

[20] T. Ed Barlow, *Small Group Ministry in the Contemporary Church* (Independence, MO: Herald Publishing, 1972), 55.

people. These exchanges are for the purposes of spiritual development and natural development. All of the relationships that people encounter develop their state of being spiritually, emotionally, and physically. Through the maturing of these relationships, people come to change and progress in their overall development. [21] The Bible echoes these same sentiments in Proverbs 13:20, "He who walks with wise men will be wise, but a companion of fools will suffer harm." Consequently, it is essential that people lend themselves to create spaces for the development of healthy relationships that improve everyone on every level. If people fail to do this, then they live out lives that are set for disappointment, destruction, and delay. People's associations are a major part of their expansion, and these associations affect their progress. It is essential that people lend themselves to producing connections that are beneficial beyond themselves.

---

[21] Barlow, 19-20

The Concept of Biblical Fellowship

The word "fellowship" is translated from the Greek *koinonia*; it refers to connection for the purpose of mutual participation.[22] In the New Testament it characteristically conveys the awareness of religious preoccupation. Eric Russ explains:

> The Biblical Greek word for fellowship is "koinonia." It is usually translated in English to "communion," "fellowship," "sharing in common" and "partake." The usage of Greek words belonging to the koin-family refer primarily, though not invariably, to *participation* in something rather than to association with others, and there is often a possessive word (genitive) to indicate that in which one participates or shares. "Sharing" or "fellowship" arises out of the common sharing of something. This is Christian fellowship: sharing together in Christ.[23]

---

[22] Donald S. Whitney, "Cultivate Koinonia," *Biblicalspirituality.org*, 2002, n.p., https://biblicalspirituality.org/wp-content/uploads/2011/01/Cultivate-Koinonia.pdf (5 February 2021).

[23] Eric Russ, "Fellowship," *Discipleshipdefined.com*, 2013, n.p., http://www.discipleshipdefined.com/resources/fellowship (5 February 2021).

Noting these factors, the concept of fellowship is connected to the discipleship of those individuals who have connected themselves to a faith community. Through the lens of biblical fellowship, leaders are able to visualize localized discipleship environments and prove the essential nature of their presence within the 21st century church through expanding modern congregational care practices in ministry.

In the biblical context, fellowship establishes a point of access to approach the exclusive influences of interconnected relationships and their role in spiritual formation, as well as natural development. The Greek word *koinonia* was used to describe organizations, industry federations, and relationships within the bounds of marriage.[24] From the usage of the word, the conclusion can be reached that "fellowship" is a word that signifies a relationship that is reliant on multiple persons. This is a mutually dependent type of relationship. The significance

---

[24] D. Whitney, n.p.

of fellowship to the church can be understood first in the point that fellowship happened instinctively as an outcome of the formation of the church.

Matthew 28:18-20 relates, "And Jesus came up and spoke to them, saying, 'All authority has been given to Me in heaven and on earth. Go therefore and make disciples of all the nations, baptizing them in the name of the Father and the Son and the Holy Spirit, teaching them to observe all that I commanded you; and lo, I am with you always, even to the end of the age." Jesus commands them to disciple. The word "disciple" is defined as the efforts to become a student or devotee. These sentiments echo the reality of one who must take action to fulfill the mandate. [25] The commands of the passage are to go, to baptize, and to teach. Discipleship was Jesus' method of developing and conditioning all those with

---

[25] Greg Herrick, "2. Understanding the Meaning of the Term 'Disciple,'" Bible.org, 11 May 2004, n.p., https://bible.org/seriespage/2-understanding-meaning-term-disciple
(20 March 2021).

whom he would come into contact during his public ministry. He invested the entirety of his ministry in a small group of twelve men. Iulian Faraoanu notes how "it is clear that the essence of the call addressed by Jesus to the future disciples lies in the invitation to take part in the movement, to join him. In other words, he invites the future disciples to leave their stable world and to embark on the journey, following the footsteps of Jesus. This is characteristic not only to Jesus' call, but to every call in the Bible, starting with the primary call of Abraham."[26]

---

[26] Iulian Faraoanu, "The Call and Mission of the Disciple in the Gospel According to Mark," *International Letters of Social and Humanistic Sciences* 60 (September 2015): 70, https://pdfs.semanticscholar.org/90e1/1c266b88bd4174e88485c0e571f73377c365.pdf?_ga=2.14100606.874651925.1613417265-309685894.1613417265 (5 February 2021).

Historical-Theological Perspective

In the New Testament, particularly in the writings of Paul, there is evidence of the assembling of people in groups. Paul uses the word *ekklesia* as "an assembly of Christians gathered for worship in a religious meeting" or as "a company of Christian, or those of who, hoping for eternal salvation through Jesus Christ, observe their own religious rites, hold their own religious meetings, and manage their own affairs, according to regulations prescribed for the body for order's sake."[27] These small groups of Christians convened frequently for the reverence of God, for reassurance, and for teaching, as early as the first periods of Christianity. However, these gatherings cannot be classified as "small groups" as they would be called today. These groups were not defined as interconnected

---

[27] Bible Study Tools, "Greek Lexicon Entry for *Ekklesia*," *The KJV New Testament Greek Lexicon*, on *Biblestudytools.com*, n.d., n.p., https://www.biblestudytools.com/lexicons/greek/kjv/ekklesia.html (3 July 2020).

groupings on a personal level to extend a tangible touch for a ministry of a large scale. These groups were the church. The church was established as a known Apostolic Movement. During the first three centuries of the church's existence, the people of God progressed as a spontaneous, interpersonal, freely-united, biological development. There were no brick-and-mortar buildings, institutions of higher learning, or establishments for the production of publications.[28]

The expansion of congregations is a biblical construct. In the Bible, groups are shown as having assembled and produced a model of impact that went beyond the confines of the local assembly. The book of Acts is the source of the small group ministry strategy. The church in Jerusalem set the precedent for what is known as the most substantial construct of developing and handling church growth on a massive scale

---

[28] Dale E. Galloway, *The Small Group Book: The Practical Guide for Nurturing Christians and Building Churches*, with Kathi Mills (Grand Rapids: Fleming H. Revell, 1995), 13-26.

without losing the intimacy of connection. Michael Morrison explains that in the beginning of Acts 1, there were 120 active converts. Moving forward into Acts 4, the number expanded to total 5,000 men. This number excluded women and children. If they were included, then the number would be far greater. Account of this is found in Acts 5:42, "And every day, in the temple and from house to house, they kept right on teaching and preaching Jesus *as* the Christ." It was common for these people to assemble in large aggregations for public worship. However, for the purpose of fellowship, there were smaller groups.

As a result, these people were able to grow spiritually because they devoted their time to studying the teachings of the apostles and to reinforcing their acquired knowledge on a more extensive level. As a component of these meetings, they spent time in fellowship and in leisure activities. Through these interactions, the believers maintained intimate bonds and the Christian community grew. The people also made it a point to worship collectively together in small group settings. They performed what have become known as ordinances, such as communion, while effectively ministering to each other.

These people were able to provide communal support in small-group settings by meeting the needs of those who were connected to them. Evangelism also was an essential component of their structure. This was the strategy that contributed to the growth and expansion of their faith community.[29] Acts 2:47 reports that they were "praising God and having favor with all the people. And the Lord was adding to their number day by day those who were being saved."

This account substantiates that small groups are biblical in their assembly, organization, and function. The small groups that were evident in the book of Acts were communities within a larger community. These groups led to the formation of the

---

[29] Michael Morrison, "Acts 1:15-26—Another Apostle is Chosen," *Gcs.edu*, 2012, n.p., https://learn.gcs.edu/mod/book/view.php?id=4475&chapterid=50 (5 February 2021).

church at large. Small groups were fulfilling the targeted areas in a ministry that was driven in purpose to worship, fellowship, disciple, minister, and evangelize. Furthermore, the John Mark Terry, *Evangelism: A Concise History* (Nashville: Broadman & Holman, 1998), 24. conclusion can be reached that effective small groups should be constructed according to this model.

A faith community is an assembly of believers who have made the conscious choice to connect with Christ. Through connecting with each other, people come to develop a deeper relationship with the Creator by extending themselves to bond with others who are made in the image and likeness of God. This kind of community is more than just family connections or simple friendships; rather, it is a place where synchronicity and understanding are developed through self-discovery through self- awareness. In this type of community, people can discover the likeness of Christ through experiencing each other as people, and through learning to appreciate individual faith- walks, as well as their importance to the diverse tapestry of faith.

Another word for this atmosphere of relationships is interconnectedness which has its foundation in the very nature of God: the Trinity. God the Father, God the Son, and God the Holy Spirit eternally subsist as one God in three persons, forever relating and loving one another. In creating us in His image, God has put this communal need in the soul of every person. Look at the story of humanity's creation. "Let us make men in our image, after our likeness" (Genesis 1:26).

People were created with an inner need to connect with each other. God makes this clear about Adam. "It is not good that the man should be alone" (Genesis 2:18). [30]

The nature of the theological construct is substantiated in the dimension of seeking an understanding of faith. Just as

---

[30] Cru, "Step 13: Establish Discipleship Relationships," *Cru.org*, n.d., n.p., https:// www.cru.org/car/en/train-and-grow/leadership-training/starting-a-ministry/growing/step-13-establish-discipleship-relationships.html (12 October 2019).

teachers must first seek an understanding of what they will teach before teaching, theologians must pursue the interpretation of what they believe or do not believe before they can progress with their clarification of theological ideas and their subsequent practical application.[31] David Schaal and Ron Harmon explain, "A good starting place is to develop a clear understanding of who we are as Community of Christ in our local neighborhoods. The church's enduring principles, grounded in the life and ministry of Jesus Christ, provide the foundation and lens through which the congregation can discern its future and respond to Christ's mission."[32] The practical principles relay competencies that are related to the

---

[31] Gerald Bray, *Biblical Interpretation: Past and Present* (Downers Grove, IL: InterVarsity Press, 1996), 511.

[32] David Schaal and Ron Harmon, eds., *Community of Christ: Pastors and Leaders Field Guide* (Independence, MO: Herald Publishing House, 2012), 8, https://www.cofchrist.org/common/cms/resources/Documents/pastors-and-leaders-field-guide.pdf (5 February 2021).

area of contemporary debates concerning identity and diversity. Themes that emerged were ideas that are linked to fundamental Christian thought and practice, such as beliefs, sensibility, and spirituality. Critical analysis, a major take-away, examined the notion of the other functions in differentiated undercurrents. These dynamics are intellectual, mental, and religious frameworks that include a focus on suggestions for scriptural pastoral ministry.[33]

Functioning as a congregational leader through the enactment of this framework, the diversity plan, in conjunction with a theologically-grounded approach for ministry, ensures that all people who plan to pursue transformation in their faith journeys are placed in an environment where they are exposed to positive beneficial relationships between people and leaders. Schaal and Harmon believe, "Christ's mission is the

---

[33] Alex D. Montoya, "Approaching Pastoral Ministry Scripturally," in *Rediscovering Pastoral Ministry: Shaping Ministry with Biblical Mandates*, ed. John MacArthur Jr. (Dallas: Word Publishing, 1995), 66.

entire reason for being a congregation. Christ's mission is not merely a ministry of the congregation, like community outreach or pastoral care. Again, mission is the entire reason for being a congregation."[34]

According to Schaal and Harmon, "The pastor and leaders of the congregation are challenged to create an environment where the above questions are the starting place for every decision and ministry of the congregation."[35] The wide selection of member- centered programs and activities benefits the understanding of ministry cultures and increases members' understanding of the world in which they live today. Awareness of spiritual principles and practical movement increases while members are at work in the world. Michael Pocock and Joseph Enriques explain that within the context of ministry, member-centered programs challenge the ministry participants to broaden perspectives, achieve cultural

---

[34] Schaal and Harmon, 7.
[35] Schaal and Harmon, 7.

enlightenment, and emphasize the importance of community among all people. As a result, from the numerous angles of opportunity presented by ministry concerning the church, a person could see that the ministry uses multicultural communities as a publicity tool to increase evangelistic efforts.[36]

Schaal and Harmon explain that the competencies of Christian education and formation in the church led to a practical application where spiritual direction became a priority coupled with active ministry that was centrally concerned with discerning the workings of God through human hands, and reinforced by necessary conversations that were both concentrated, yet spiritual, in nature. Schaal and Harmon state, "Creating this 'new community' in a society that places an emphasis on individual satisfaction and choice is challenging. Many Christians shuffle between churches and denominations

---

[36] Michael Pocock and Joseph Henriques, Cultural Change and Your Church: Helping Your Church Thrive in a Diverse Society (Grand Rapids: Baker Books, 2002), 196.

in search of what best meets their needs. A mission-shaped congregation is not about meeting the individual preferences of its members. A mission-shaped congregation is about coming together to become like Christ for the sake of the world."[37] Developing a ministry framework positions the developers to engage and explore the temperament of spiritual direction. The knowledge is positioned to build the ministry framework strategically from a communal perspective, and to provide intersecting access points through engagement via interest in small group dynamics. Through the framework's design, there are also allowances to embrace diverse opportunities to connect with congregants and people from all occupations to enact spiritual guidance in congregational ministry. Pocock and Henriques report that being actively engaged in ministry, through this framework, allows the leadership and the participant to grow together. Because of these connections, the ministry can assist people as they

---

[37] Schaal and Harmon, 7-8.

transition from their own intensive lifestyles and formation experiences in the world toward increased responsibility for expediting, emboldening, and establishing the training and formation experiences of others.[38] A ministry makes strides to reflect diversity in principle and practice through its diversity statement, which reflects the motivation to make improvements in quality of life via the community and members to which the ministry provides services. The diversity statement makes clear the stance that there are no barriers concerning participation in any ministry-related activities, particularly in the small group framework. The diversity statement sheds light on, and ties its many forms back into, the central mission of the church at its core. The ministry, as a whole, seeks to maintain a shared environment that not only attracts people, but also retains them.[39]The goal of the diversity plan for ministry, when implemented through the

---

[38] Pocock and Henriques, 195.
[39] Pocock and Henriques, 180.

small group framework, is to prepare members to engage effectively in the areas of interconnectivity and congregational relationship. In addition to the mutual respect among all classifications of people, there is a thrust to promote a mutual value for all cultural backgrounds, to break the power of stereotypes and misjudgments, and to provide experiences of purposeful faith-centered interaction.

Cultural and Personal Perspective

The task is to implement a framework that is holistically sufficient, theologically sound, and efficient in implantation to the congregation. The framework of ministry, focusing specifically on the small-group dynamic, assists in the construction of the congregation's knowledge as a faith community and in developing them individually, while placing emphasis on enhancing social awareness and skill acquisition. Within the framework, the over-arching efforts of pastoral leadership is to increase the members' level of knowledge, enhance their leadership skills, develop more leaders, and expand the members' awareness through creating constructive environments for ministry that are successfully supported by collaboration.

In regard to my cultural context, I am a duly consecrated Bishop within the Full Gospel Baptist Church. Currently, I serve as the Third Presiding Bishop of the Full Gospel Baptist Church Fellowship, International, which was founded by

Pastor Bishop Paul S. Morton, Sr., and was led by Bishop J. Warren Walker. In the Full Gospel Baptist Church Fellowship, I have served in many capacities, including Chairman of the Tehillah Music Group. I am a highly motivated minister, mentor, counselor, speaker, and spiritual father. Additionally, I am also the founder and organizer of L. L. Brandon Ministries, Inc.

In addition to these, my denominational foundation is rooted in the "right of choice." This is a freedom that is substantiated in the perspective that the Gospel of Jesus Christ is expanded by affirming the full free expression of the gifts of the Spirit pertaining to the Body of Christ. The Fellowship is persuaded that the choice to execute the implementation of these spiritual gifts is a priority for the local New Testament Church to function fully as the dynamic organism that God has intended. Through teaching servant-leaders, there is the realization that pastors and ministry leaders comprise the frontline and face of ministry. As teachers and leaders serving in various capacities, the reality is that they may only have a particular member for a month, a year, or maybe longer. Nevertheless, no matter the length of their engagement and interaction, they are a connecting point. Rachel R. Van Der Stuyf explains, "In scaffolding instruction a more knowledgeable other provides scaffolds or supports to facilitate the learner's development."[40] Leaders are the scaffolds for development. As servant-leaders, practitioners are connecting to other ministry programming that extends across the church for applied knowledge and active plans that will assist communities of faith to grow people and to develop greater leaders for the church.

The University of Houston points out, "Constructivism is a theory, based on observation and scientific study, about how people learn."[41] People who seek to become part of a faith

---

[40] Rachel R. Van Der Stuyf, "Scaffolding as a Teaching Strategy," Adolescent Learning and Development 52, no. 3 (2002): 2, http://ateachingpath1.weebly.com/uploads/1/7/8/9/17892507/stuyf_2002.pdf (5 January 2021).

[41] University of Houston, "About Constructivism," Uh.edu, n.d., n.p., https:// uh.edu/charter-school/about-us/about-constructivism/ (5 February 2021).

community are looking for a place to "construct their own understanding and knowledge" of God, "through experiencing things and reflecting on those experiences" in their individual faith journeys. When people encounter something new in any religious communal setting, they have to resolve this with their previously-learned concepts and experiences. As a result, this may guide people toward transforming what they believe, or toward discarding the obsolete information as a reference point in moving forward in the journey ahead.[42] As a member of a faith community, even as a senior leader and visionary, the recognizable factor is that each member is an active architect of his or her own knowledge. To do this, the individual must pose questions, investigate, and evaluate what this person recognizes. Therefore, the theoretical approach to ministry is constructivism. This theory echoes the sentiments of creating spaces where people are allowed to engage information, to grow, and to create their experiences that bring

---

[42] University of Houston, n.p.

them closer to God, while connecting with people in the process. The most rewarding part of constructivism is the constant growth that takes place when the individual achieves success, experiences a life transition for the better, and gains understanding.

Scaffolding theory is relevant to ministry frameworks because it speaks to the intentional efforts of providing support through transition, learning, the acquisition of new life skills, and functional post-learning processes. Soviet psychologist Lev Vygotsky is widely known as the innovative mind behind the theory of scaffolding. Scaffolding theory is inclusive of all necessary structural supports that are concentrated in the areas of social interaction and instruction. Janet Maybin, Neil Mercer, and Barry Stierer believe, "For something to count as scaffolding it has to relate to a task prescribed in relation to a specific learning goal that a learner is not yet able to succeed in unaided, where the scaffolding has been designed specifically to bridge the task demand in the light of the learners' current level, and where it actually allows the learner to be more successful than would have been possible otherwise."[43] These supports are compared to the supports that are found alongside buildings as they are being constructed. The scaffolding supports the formation of new concepts and information that are learned for advancement; the scaffolding is removed after competencies have been proven proficient within the individual, and when the content is completely understood.

Instructional scaffolding, also known as "Vygotsky scaffolding" or just "scaffolding," is a teaching method that helps people learn by working alongside individuals who assist them through phases of development by providing stability and support. The central tenet of this theory is that more can be accomplished this way than compared to learning

---

[43] Janet Maybin, Neil Mercer, and Barry Stierer, "'Scaffolding': Learning in the Classroom," in Thinking Voices: The Work of the National Oracy Project, ed. Kate Norman (London: Hodder & Stoughton, 1992), 188.

in an independent manner. Scaffolding allows the individual to learn and acquire knowledge in a supportive communal setting that is found in ministry models, namely, small groups. I. Verenikina reports, "Gordon Wells referred to scaffolding as a way of operationalising Vygotsky's . . . concept of working in the zone of proximal development' . . . . He identified three important features that give educational scaffolding its particular character: 1) the essentially dialogic nature of the discourse in which knowledge is co-constructed; 2) the significance of the kind of activity in which knowing is embedded and 3) the role of artefacts that mediate knowing . . . ."[44] A general consensus is that participants learn more when collaborating with others who have a wider range of skills and knowledge than the participants currently have. These instructors are the "scaffolding" that helps the person expand

---

[44] I. Verenikina, "Scaffolding and Learning: Its Role in Nurturing New Learners,"
Ro.uow.edu.au, May 2008, 163,
https://ro.uow.edu.au/cgi/viewcontent.cgi?article=1043&context=edupapers (5 February 2021).

their learning boundaries and learn more than they would be able to on her own."

Considering the above theories, behaviorism and existentialism are two philosophies that influence the functionality of small groups and their subsequent designs across the world. Existentialism holds the stance that "the nature of a man's existence or being is that man is completely free. Man's condition of freedom connotes more than the simple free will versus determinism issue . . . ."[45] These two philosophies affect the church world in such areas as curriculum, methods of teaching, effectiveness, discipleship, and progress. These two philosophies were developed from, and are based on, the research of creative, yet innovative minds, who dared to gain understanding of a true educational experience and development.

Behaviorism is naturalistic. The idea and concepts of

---

[45] Kenneth P. Hillner, History and Systems of Modern Psychology: A Conceptual Approach (New York: Gardner Press, 1984), 258.

behaviorism were made known by such innovative minds as Ivan Pavlov, B. F. Skinner, Edward Thorndike, John Watson, and Clark Hull. George Graham explains that "Loosely speaking, behaviorism is an attitude—a way of conceiving of empirical constraints on psychological state attribution. Strictly speaking, behaviorism is a doctrine—a way of doing psychological or behavioral science itself."[46] Conditioning occurs as a result of interacting with the environment. Interaction with the environment is an extremely important concept when referring to the philosophy of behaviorism. Kendra Cherry explains that in the behaviorism school of thought, ". . . behavior can be studied in a systematic and observable manner with no consideration of internal mental states."[47] In other words, it can be observed without the

---

[46] George Graham, "Behaviorism," The Stanford Encyclopedia of Philosophy, Spring 2019 ed., ed. Edward N. Zalta, n.p., https://plato.stanford.edu/archives/spr2019/ entries/behaviorism/ (5 February 2021).

[47] Kendra Cherry, "History and Key Concepts of Behavioral Psychology," Verywellmind.com, 20 February 2021, n.p., http://psychology.about.com/od/

consideration of the "state of mind" of a particular individual. Within the area of behaviorism, there are two categories of conditioning: classical and operant. Kahn Academy notes, "In classical conditioning, the stimuli that *precede* a behavior will vary . . . to alter that behavior . . . . In operant conditioning, the consequences which come *after* a behavior will vary, to alter that behavior."[48] Small discipleship groups in the church can be used in this way, shaping both behavior and culture in their respective dynamics.

Behaviorism is completely the opposite of existentialism. The simplest comparison/contrast between the two would be that the behaviorist believes that behavior is caused by environmental conditions. According to Gerald E. Zuriff, "Behaviorism makes certain assumptions about human behavior and the working of the mind."[49] David Cohen

---

behavioralpsychology/f/behaviorism.htm (15 March 2021).
[48] Kahn Academy, "Classical and Operant Conditioning Article," Khanacademy. org, n.d., n.p., https://www.khanacademy.org/test-prep/mcat/behavior/learning-slug/a/ classical-and-operant-conditioning-article (5 February 2021).
[49] Gerald E. Zuriff, Behaviorism: A Conceptual Reconstruction (New

explains, "The central tenet of behaviorism is that thoughts, feelings, and intentions, mental processes all, do not determine what we do. Our behavior is the product of our conditioning. We are biological machines and do not consciously act; rather we react to stimuli."[50]

They were continually devoting themselves to the apostles' teaching and to fellowship, to the breaking of bread and to prayer. Everyone kept feeling a sense of awe; and many wonders and signs were taking place through the apostles. And all the believers were together and had all things in common; and they *began* selling their property and possessions and were sharing them with all, as anyone might have need. Day by day continuing with one mind in the temple, and breaking bread from house to house, they were taking their meals together with gladness and sincerity of heart, praising God and having favor with all the people. And the Lord was adding to their

---

York: Columbia University Press, 1985), 687.
[50] David Cohen, "Behaviorism," The Oxford Companion to the Mind, ed. Richard
L. Gregory (New York: Oxford University Press, 1987), 71.

number day by day those who were being saved. (Acts 2:42-47)

They met for worship and teaching in the temple, but they also met in smaller settings, such as homes, for the purpose of developing community. Four attributes were given that describe what they were devoted to on a regular basis: the Apostles' Doctrine (the Word of God), fellowship, prayer that was inclusive of worship, and breaking bread together. Each church must thoroughly examine the culture of its ministry and communities. Small group facilitators and ministry strategists must realize that the small discipleship group curriculum and culture are tied to the culture of their community and society. These small groups must really analyze every aspect and detail, because the diversity of the ministry is often representative of the diversity within the community.

Just as there are different problems and needs in the small groups, the same lie within the community. Small groups being "microcosms," they shape the church into a community and give it a sense of unity and togetherness. The ultimate result is creating productive citizens with a heart for community, a love of God, and the advancement of society. Indeed, church is one of the "microcosms" of society. Robert T. Carter, Tamara R. Buckley, and Schekeva P. Hall stipulate, "Liberty, democracy, domestic tranquility, economic prosperity, and all the other benefits traditionally associated with American society require an educated people. Ensuring the development of that educated populace"[51] is the sole purpose of public ministry. The small group's role is not simply to serve the students, but to serve the community. In the current era, America faces immense change in every aspect. According to Bill Hull, "The change to a churchocentric discipling model required a community relationship, a shared discipling among several people."[52]

---

[51] Robert T. Carter, Tamara R. Buckley, and Schekeva P. Hall, "Racial Harassment in American Schools," in Handbook of School Counseling, ed. Hardin L. K. Coleman and Christine Yeh (New York: Routledge, 2011), 111.

[52] Bill Hull, The Disciple-Making Church: Leading a Body of Believers on the Journey of Faith (Grand Rapids, MI: Fleming H. Revell, 1990),

Making disciples can be accomplished most effectively in a small group setting. Jesus said to be "teaching them to observe all that I commanded you" (Matt 28:20). However, this can be realized best in a small group setting.[53] The relationship between the church and society is extremely important. In Ho Jei explains, "Small group ministry can expose the nature of community of a church. It is because a small group is a community and a church is a community. The direction of small group leadership development has to turn toward making divine communities, in which genuine fellowship with Christ and other Christians can be experienced, through the small group leaders."[54]

The small group concept can be used to make churches so much better. A sense of community can be encouraged by creating diverse sets of activities that give people the chance to explore purpose and to grow in their relationship with

---

25.
[53] Hull, 25.
[54] Jei, 22

Christ. Of course, there is ever more to do. No one is more aware of the challenges that are still unmet than are the citizens in their individual communities. Carter, Buckley, and Hall believe that the ultimate success of authentic discipleship processes and the establishment of community will depend upon instilling the principles of community, as well as ". . .liberty, democracy, domestic tranquility, economic prosperity, and all the other benefits traditionally associated with"[55] Christian principles and practices.

The subject of the curriculum, or the structure, would be established on the work of Jean Piaget. Piaget developed a theory of cognitive development that moved beyond a teacher/leader simply giving information. Carol Garhart Mooney expresses it this way: "Many adults still hold the notion that a teacher is someone who shares information.

Using Piaget's theory about children's learning requires changing the image of *teacher* into someone who nurtures

---

[55] Carter, Buckley, and Hall, 111.

inquiry and supports the children's own search for answers."[56] The process is the same when configuring small discipleship groups within the appropriate contexts. In these group settings, people learn best as active participants in their experiences and opportunities. These are executed by giving the participants the guidance, the materials, and the space that they need to explore the world around them completely. Small group settings encourage people to ask and to answer questions, as well as to make meaningful connections for themselves. People learn through large and small projects that explore themes or topics, that are discussed, and that cut across numerous life experiences. Small groups are collaborative, which develops social skills, and which yield educational discoveries that empower people with a sense of accomplishment, satisfaction, and joy about new experiences and growth.[57]

---

[56] Carol Garhart Mooney, Theories of Childhood: An Introduction to Dewey, Montessori, Erikson, Piaget & Vygotsky (St. Paul, MN: Redleaf, 2000), 62.

[57] Robert Evans, The Human Side of School Change: Reform,

Collaboration is a vital element in all small group settings. It is working together as a team to benefit all involved. Looking into the future, collaboration with the participants will be the most important team you can create as a facilitator or designer. Community support is essential in the development of people. Collaboration should also occur between each member of the group and facilitators. Diversity is important to focus on within the church's small group settings because it is another viewpoint group leader must deal with. The churches are no longer predominately white, non-handicapped people, but a mix of many different cultures, ethnicities, and handicaps. People can learn from each other, especially when individuals come from a variety of backgrounds, so leaders must take advantage of such a wonderful opportunity by acknowledging differences within their teachings.

Small groups should give participants a greater understanding

---

Resistance, and the Real-Life Problems of Innovation (San Francisco: Jossey-Bass, 1996), 21-27.

of the world around them and their potential to contribute to it. Small groups reinforce and advocate the idea of progressive education. John Dewey suggests that ". . . traditional education as just described, was beyond the scope of young learners." Progressive education as described by Dewey should include socially engaging learning experiences that are developmentally appropriate for young children."[58] These settings encourage participants to take an active hands-on approach that would teach children to identify problems or questions, investigate them, and ultimately arrive at important conclusions for themselves.

Dewey's phrase "learning by doing" is a hallmark of the progressive approach,[59] and this approach is found in many contemporary progressive ministries today. Instead of simply embracing and accepting knowledge that is handed down by

---

[58] Morgan K. Williams, "John Dewey in the 21st Century," Journal of Inquiry and Action in Education 9, no. 1 (2017): 92, https://digitalcommons.buffalostate.edu/cgi/viewcontent.cgi?article=1147&context=jiae (5 February 2021).
[59] Williams, 93.

others, small group settings ensure that people develop important thinking and social skills that will benefit them throughout their lives, and will benefit them as productive members of society. As a progressive ministry, small groups embrace hands-on learning and teaching. People are not just taught important knowledge and biblical practice, but they are also taught the skills to obtain knowledge and how to rightly apply it to produce tangible evidence in their lives. People will explore, discover, collaborate, and learn through a project-based curriculum and scenarios. Each person brings unique skills, experiences, and learning styles to the group. Accordingly, small groups use a rich variety of teaching methods, including visual and sensory materials, to help all people learn. By doing this, the participants draw on their own experiences, interests, and abilities. The progressive education plan and philosophy within these small groups includes an integrated curriculum that is focused on themes.

The small group setting carries a strong emphasis on problem-solving and critical thinking, the development of social skills, and understanding and action as the goals of learning, as opposed to the simple repetition of rote knowledge. Transition is something that must be considered when dealing with people in small group settings. A group facilitator should never just allow a person with special needs to leave one major area of life and transition into the next without assisting and planning for the student. New environments can make a person highly anxious and nervous, and lack of support from a familiar environment or person can make the experience a bad one. Small group designers and facilitators must prepare participants to be comfortable with transitions, so they can have experiences that are more pleasurable in life and ministry.

The black church has viewed the small group approach as a "white church" strategy that does not fit what people deem as the traditional model for their contexts. Small groups have been integrated into the fabric of the black church community in an effort to keep larger and smaller churches together alike. In the present-day experience, small groups in the black church need to exemplify several key factors in order to work successfully in tandem with the ministry model. The leadership must be "all-in," small groups must be infused into the mission and vision of the ministry, and small groups need to be a way of life and not just a ministry. Small groups are "space-contextualized," and they must be marketed well.

Small discipleship groups that are successful in the black church dynamic are very intentional about where they meet. They consist of diverse people with various backgrounds and lifestyles. Some groups meet at restaurants, via Zoom video conferencing, or in homes. Others choose spaces that are unconventional and outside what would be considered as the norm. However, the success of these groups in the black church setting relies heavily on appropriate contextualization.

Small Group and Ministry Models

There are several small group models that are available to be implemented in various settings. Each type has its advantages and disadvantages. These group types can be implemented in diverse congregations to achieve the desired effect that is gauged by ministry initiatives and congregational care efforts. Open small groups are viable for visitors and new members. The majority of these groups continue to have open enrollment, thereby signifying that there is no cap to the quantity of attendees who desire to become part of this type of group. New people can feel free to join at any time. Some of these groups will begin an expansion process for a new group once a certain number of regular attendees is attained. There are other types of group models that stop accepting new members once the group has become a certain size. Open groups are the most preferred as they are welcoming in nature and they continually present the opportunity to "add one more," presenting the continuous manifestation of expansion.

The advantages found in open groups are that they are centered on outreach, and they are beneficial in the strategy of rapid growth. These groups are intentionally evangelism-focused, and they encourage interconnectivity. Open small groups afford the opportunity for flexibility and freedom within each small group's ministry. Even with the advantages, the disadvantage in open small groups is in regard to obtaining a meaningful level of closeness, responsibility, and protection. If not structured and capped at a certain number, open groups can expand to a size that breaks the community quality of a small- group experience. Also, open groups often do not encourage an intentional degree of dedication.[60]

Closed small groups restrain the number of participants in order to concentrate on fostering an atmosphere of confidence and relationship among group members. Once a group commences, new members and visitors are commonly

---

[60] Glen Martin and Gary McIntosh, Creating Community: Deeper Fellowship through Small Group Ministry (Nashville: Broadman & Holman, 1997), 86

deterred from attending meetings. Closed groups usually assemble for a particular interval of time before making spots available to new members. The advantages of closed groups are that the expectations of the members are prominent when it comes to discipleship and spiritual growth. Additionally, closed groups present an occasion for deeper points of reliance and duty. Closed groups, by their nature, demand an intense level of commitment from their members. The disadvantages of closed groups are that the structure can obstruct the routine of interpersonal evangelism— "going after" friends and family—because they are excluded from joining. Some leaders believe that closed groups have an affinity to become inner-directed or fixated, which can eventually lead to factions, idle chatter, and unpleasantness. Closed groups offer an opening for greater amounts of trust and mutual fidelity. To conclude, closed groups do not provide much pliability for the general small- groups ministry.[61]

---

[61] Martin and McIntosh, 40

The cell group model views small groups as the rudimentary components of a church assembly, much like a biological cellular unit is a simple element of a human body. Thus, small groups are not handled as "one setting among the masses," but are considered as essential. Four vital items make up the "DNA" of a cell group: devotion, teaching, social evangelism, and discipleship. If these groups are functioning in their proper capacity, then each cell group will produce and increase on its own, reassigning these like qualities from group to group. Cell groups usually have between five and fifteen members. They prefer to meet weekly, in addition to having outside fellowships between meetings. The advantage of this type of group is that it is deliberate about building active disciples of Christ. Cell groups are a realistic and operative means to form a culture of discipleship within a local church setting. Cell groups' rallying point spotlights personal evangelism, and they are a confirmed technique to enlarge the kingdom of God. The disadvantage of the cell group model is that promoting the magnitude of small groups outside other ministries sometimes causes cell groups to remove themselves from the rest of the church and become inaccessible. When the organization of a cell group is unplanned, then it can be an effort that yields no results for an inclusive small-groups ministry. To conclude, the emphasis on evangelism and statistical growth can possibly regulate the level of belief and understanding within a group.

The concept of small groups, or cell groups, is not a new phenomenon in ministry strategy. Upon personal observation, they have become essential components of modern ministry culture. There are ministries, at present, that define themselves through the orchestration of their small group ministries. These are not divisive mechanisms; rather, they constitute an essential dynamic that creates parts of a whole relationship. On the other end of the spectrum, there are other ministries that depend on small groups to assist in facilitating growth within their local assemblies. In some ministry models, small groups are used in church-planting efforts as an extension of a ministry. The overall goal of this strategic approach is to make disciples who are informed, engaged, active, disciplined, and willing to be developed. These groups carry the responsibility and the mandate of the church that is reflected in the core of the Great Commission.

From Luke 10:27, one is able to understand the meaning and purpose of areas that are essential to effective ministry, which are learning, serving others, and obtaining spiritual growth. Small groups have been essential in creating and maintaining a tangible presence and connectivity in small and large ministries. Small groups are essential in creating circles of relationship. The main objective behind every effort in this ministry strategy is to lead people into a relationship with Jesus Christ that transforms them. Small cell groups give congregants an opportunity to engage and to extend themselves into the opportunity to develop meaningful relationships. By developing these meaningful relationships, the process of transformation is initiated, and biblical principles become tangible realities in the lives of the believer. Small groups are a better place to process spiritual truths and to learn what following Jesus looks like.

The mega-church model can be quite intimidating to newcomers in the faith, or even to those who are experienced in church culture. In this modern day, it is easy to get lost in the theatrics and in mega numbers. There are some individuals who can feel isolated or even disconnected in the midst of a ministry that seems to have so much to offer. Small groups afford people of all walks of life an opportunity to see the necessity of God in addressing individual and collective needs. They can show the personal intimacy that is needed to provide solutions and needed services in a way that might be a struggle for a large congregation.

Ministry Models

The purpose of this review is to support the project in regard to determining small group participants' perspectives about the process of implementing these groups, as well as their integration into various ministries' congregational care practices. The literature highlights complications, uncertainties, and insights that growing ministries face, as well as leaders' experiences when attempting to integrate effectively small groups and perspectives toward them as a whole. The primary goal of this review is to highlight the most significant variables, which are the participants, their perspectives, and the individual nature of this enhancing ministerial practice.

John E. Jones presents, "The major objectives of a T- or training group are awareness and skill building. The objectives center around helping the individual participants to grow in increased awareness of their feeling experience, of their reaction to other people, of their impact on other people, of how others impact them, and in their awareness of how people interrelate and of how groups operate."[62] Creating cultures to disciple members in the 21st century church is a task that has proven to be a priority within any ministry that seeks to expand and to leave a lasting impact. Discipleship is the main objective through which ministers seek to teach people the disciplines of the faith for the betterment of themselves and their community of faith. Discipleship, in its essence, is an unwavering requirement for continual spiritual growth that garners a place of maturity within the life of the believer. People who become connected to ministries come from diverse backgrounds and experiences.[63] As a result, these experiences sometimes carry intense emotional issues, and people have developed barriers that have proven difficult to

---

[62] John E. Jones, "Types of Growth Groups," in The Pfeiffer Library, vol. 13, 2nd ed. (San Francisco: Jossey-Bass/Pfeiffer, 1998), 2

[63] [2]Albert H. Epp, *Discipleship Therapy: Healthy Christians, Healthy Churches* (Henderson, NE: Stairway Discipleship, 1993), 228.

overcome. Through active discipleship via interpersonal groups, participants are able to engage in a series of chances to access guidance through instruction, development through engagement in active processes, and direct attention that focuses on cultivation.

Interpersonal groups are a key to sustaining the vitality and connectivity of churches of all sizes. The dynamics of these groups are rendered effective through the nature of establishing essential relationships that put people in direct contact with other individuals from diverse backgrounds. These groups are collaborative and empowering in nature through the promotion of affirmation. Participants in these group settings are able to obtain information, accountability partners, and a mutual support system to assist in navigating through life's transitions, which take many forms. John L. Casteel states, "You belong to an intimate band of men and women, who knew they had been lifted right out of their old life into a new life, and who met together to listen to the

Scriptures, or the letters written to them by their leaders; to pray; and to eat together at the table of their Lord."[64] The importance of maintaining interpersonal groups is that it allows individuals to engage people outside their normal associations, as well as establish diverse connections for the betterment of their faith communities.

The 21st century church has made significant strides to promote the growth of congregations and to provide contingency measures for reaching every classification of person found in the membership of congregations. The church has become an environment that promotes life, excitement, innovation, and ingenuity. The collaborative environment inspires members to create new ways to create change and to move in a progressive manner towards the future. Ministries are comprised of different models and sub-structures. Miguel Angel Cerna declares, "When a large group divides into

---

[64] John L. Casteel, *Spiritual Renewal Through Personal Groups* (New York: Association Press, 1957), 21.

smaller ones, each individual can receive better care and more personal attention from group leaders and other members."[65] The small group component is an active approach taken by ministries to provide an atmosphere of intimacy where people are made accessible without the presence of intimidation, inferiority, or shame. The mutual grounds for sharing are opportunities for the participants to create solutions and to till the ground for potential keys to confront disparities that are found within the community in which they live.

Small groups have always been an influential factor in church growth and development. They have provided the foundational components to extend the tangible reach of the church and the various initiatives that ministries enact for the betterment of their communities. Small groups capitalize on the strengths found in the group setting. Participants come from all walks of life and different demographics. Within these

---

[65] Miguel Angel Cerna, *The Power of Small Groups in the Church* (Newbury Park, CA: El Camino, 1991), 21.

demographics are people with various subsets of abilities and strengths that can prove to be transformative in nature. Small groups are a necessity for the identification of new leaders and the cultivation of all members who actively participate. Cerna relates that "Each person also gets more individualized recognition and his or her soul-winning abilities can be developed and channeled into creative witnessing activities."[66] Cerna provides insight into the importance of establishing environments where people can learn from each other. These are instances when valuable knowledge is transmitted to benefit the growth of people on a comprehensive scale. The essentials that small groups bring to the ministry setting are invaluable, and they allow in-reach to be effective, while embracing those who are coming in to join the ministry from the outside. Active ministry developers should be mindful that they place people first in their efforts to address needs in a

---

[66] Cerna, 21.

direct manner through intimate settings that will provide a necessary place of refuge that is being sought out on a continual basis.

Every church will not be large or be a mega-church. Throughout the nation, there are small churches comprised of members who are dedicated to Christ, to the call, and to the Great Commission. The small church has proven to be effective in maintaining the intimacy of worship, connectivity, and relationship. Carl S. Dudley emphasizes the conversion of small groups into effective ministries that engage congregants on a more personal level due to their size.[67] These small churches have shown that size is not an indicator of success, but rather the quality of the relational dynamic that leads to the success of ministry overall.

Small churches, ranging in size from about 100 to 200

---

[67] Carl S. Dudley, *Effective the Small Churches in the Twenty-First Century*
(Nashville: Abingdon Press, 2003), 15-16.

members, can remain relevant through continual advancement in creating places for people to grow in comfortable settings. Smaller congregations prove to be less intimidating by allowing all members' presence to be felt and carry a noticeable significance to the culture of the established faith community. The members of these small churches play multiple roles in order to sustain the work of the ministry. Dudley speaks to the fact that many members take on more than one role within the ministry, which allows for cross-training, visibility, flexibility, and fluidity. The nature of a small ministry forges teams of people who work together in cooperation and who foster the bonds of mutuality towards the pursuit of a common cause. Small church congregations reflect some similarities with small group settings. The small church invests its resources in creating leadership and members with dual or multifaceted capabilities to maintain the ministry's progressive thrust and relevance. Dudley presents small churches as a "single cell" associations that "are not organizational errors to be corrected, but intentional choices of members who put a priority on human relationships."[68] He explains that the "small church is an association that generates and lives by its social capital."[69] Furthermore, the small church is "a *single cell* of caring that includes the whole congregation."[70] In concurrence with small groups, Dudley portrays the small church and its construction as essential to understanding the foundations of smaller groups on a larger scale within larger ministries. These smaller churches parallel the intimacies of small groups that allow ministries, even lesser in size, to build something bigger while still maintaining authentic relationships with parishioners.[71]

People enter ministries with the expectation to be received, and they seek to become part of a place where they belong.

---

[68] Dudley, 11.

[69] Dudley, 29.

[70] Dudley, 40.

[71] Dudley, 55.

Fellowship has always been essential to the development of understanding between people, and fellowship creates the climate for relationships to be constituted. Bill Donahue and Russ Robison "The small group ministry in a church rises and falls on the quality of its leaders."[72] Small groups can be beneficial to ministries across the board, regardless of size. If the church is relatively big, then small groups can assist with the church's vision being perceptible and within reach of the members of the congregation.[73] For ministries that are seeking to undertake exponential growth and become evangelistic in nature, small groups can provide the substantial momentum to increase outreach efforts that bring people in and give them a reason to stay. Donahue's and Robison's assessment of the matter claims that small groups are essentially effective for

---

[72] Bill Donahue and Russ Robinson, *Building a Church of Small Groups: A Place Where Nobody Stands Alone* (Grand Rapids: Zondervan, 2001), 123.

[73] Donahue and Robinson, 12.

ongoing discipleship opportunities that strengthen both new converts and the people who have been in the faith for a significant amount of time. The success lies with the leader's ability to develop, discern, and execute plans to move the groups forward.[74]

The inclusion of small groups within the setting of the local congregation should be paced and systematic. The structure should be combined with the appropriate leader who has congregational care experience that carries passion, mission, and charisma for growing people in body, mind, and spirit. Building small groups affords the ministry the chance to link the resources to people in order to meet their needs. For sustainability of these groups, ongoing training and assessment are paramount to ensure continually that efforts are strategically aligned with the mission of the ministry, and to ensure effectiveness to the members of the congregation that

---

[74] Donahue and Robinson, 105-116.

these groups serve. Merit should be given to the fact that building a church is predicated on the building of the people. As the people obtain growth and opportunities to expand themselves, the changing aspects of ministry will shift to create a climate where all people can be received.

Randy Frazee presents a model for building Christian community. He holds the perspective that "The development of meaningful relationships where every member carries a significant sense of belonging is central to what it means to be the church."[75]14 Frazee's vision for compelling groups is based on the foundation of regaining biblical community. He discusses the issue of the church moving beyond small groups and creating interconnected communities. A community's strengths lie within the diversity of the people and in being close-knit.[76] The bigger that they become, the more likely the

---

[75] Randy Frazee, *The Connecting Church: Beyond Small Groups to Authentic Community* (Grand Rapids: Zondervan, 2001), 35
[76] Frazee, 56-59.

chance that distance may occur if the ideals are not sustained. Frazee argues that isolation is "the second major obstacle to connecting in true community. This contemporary human condition flows out of the first major obstacle, namely, a culture of individualism, which promises to give us the best—only to inflict on us the disease of loneliness."[77] No matter how big a church may become, it should never lose the idea of community or its essential focus. Authentic community requires a level of intimacy that can be lost as expansion happens. Therefore, intentional times of fellowship and connectivity must be created to sustain the bonds in a healthy way as growth takes place.

These small groups cultivate deeper friendships that, over time, mature into places of sure accountability. People not only become acquainted in these settings, but they come to know the transparency of others' lives, and people are able to walk

---

[77] Frazee, 110.

through life's various transitions without judging the temporary circumstances that surround an individual's place of change. Small groups are an opportunity for people to engage each other up close, while dealing with real-life problems as they are, and not as people want them to appear to be. Frazee challenges the reader to identify with the principle of bringing out the best in others through direct accountability and encouragement. [78] These groups require maximum participation, and they provide a platform to discuss relevant topics within the church among trusted individuals who will nurture as well as sustain communal inclusivity. It is critical that churches maintain a posture that substantiates confidence-building and liberation toward progressive life change. Understanding that these groups take on various forms in a series of countless settings, change becomes the fabric of the culture. As a result, people are prompted to seek out continual self- improvement that is both spiritual and natural

---

[78] Frazee, 138.

in nature.

Churches across the nation are consistently attempting to develop new ways to prepare their ministries for the onset of drastic change. The needs of both the communities and the people that they serve are continually changing. In efforts to pace ministries and to apply resources in the most intentional manner, churches are taking the time to assess the strengths and weaknesses of their ministry models. George discusses the need for the church to take an active approach in modernizing ministry efforts and implementing unconventional approaches to give the ministry an advanced yet competitive edge. Both millennials and older members of congregations require a sense of belonging. Creating this sense of belonging will prompt members to invest in and to become part of an entity in which there is a solidified relationship of reciprocity. George engages the dialogue concerning the readiness of the church to make a strategic effort to update ministries in teaching, discipleship, and growth efforts.[79] Jei explains that "There are four dimensions of ministry that a cell could accomplish: loving (pastoral care), learning (Bible knowledge), deciding (internal administration), and doing (duties that serve those outside the group)."[80]

Since small groups have arrived on the modern church scene, the idea has emerged that corporate worship experiences are not enough to maintain the strong bonds of fellowship or to promote growth within the local congregation. Explicitly, the use of the small groups must be aligned with the vision and strategic goals of the ministry in order to create effective change in the lives of members of the congregation. It is imperative that churches consider adapting new ways to connect the people in their congregation with each other through establishing familial relationships that assist in churches always remaining tangible and never out of reach.

---

[79] George, 89.
[80] Jei, 104.

Today's church must take the radical approach and extend itself beyond conventional means to become relevant forces in the world to address the real-life issues of the people whom they serve.

Evangelism has always been the most central mandate and mission through which the good news of the gospel is spread. Michael P. Green highlights that evangelism should be at the forefront of a church's efforts to move outward and to expand the knowledge of God by bringing it directly to where the people are located. Ho Kung Kim summarizes Green's thinking as, "God, through His Spirit, leads His evangelists very carefully."[81] Evangelism should be a natural priority within the church setting to reinforce the practicality of The Great Commission. Too many ministries are inclined to preoccupy all their efforts by focusing on the interior of the

---

[81] Ho Kyung Kim, "The Biblical Approach to Church Growth through Personal Evangelism" (D.Min. proj., Liberty Baptist Theological Seminary, 2000), 28.

local ministry setting, instead of reaching out towards the people. Churches can become satisfied with growth by way of individuals who may connect with the ministry through transfer, and never extend themselves to soul-winning and subsequent discipleship. Churches are increasing in numerical growth. However, these churches are not evangelizing in the truest sense. They are simply gaining members who transfer in or are simply "swapping" members because of their longing not to settle to and become invested in any particular local church, but would rather switch from church to church to suit their yearnings. Churches may also encounter people who find themselves at a different church every couple of years for reasons such as relocation, doctrine, and philosophy of ministry.

It must be considered that evangelism does take place within the small group setting. The small group provides members with the opportunity to discover, rediscover, and receive answers to questions that they may have. Large settings may be intimidating to members who may ask for information that is specific to their individual faith journeys. The church has to be conscious that evangelism remains the focus, and not to misinterpret the fact that the church is evangelistic. Churches that are strong are interconnected and evangelistic in nature, because evangelism is a regimented practice through which people become bearers of both spiritual and natural fruit. Evangelism actively wins souls to the kingdom, spreads the influence of the gospel, and provides an essential gateway for the church to take an active role in the spiritual growth of the believer. Evangelism renders both the actions and the teachings of the church effective by becoming meshed with the life of the believer through all developmental stages.

Addressing the needs of the unchurched is a landscape that is changing in the religious world. The unchurched demographic does not just consist of people who are unbelievers, but also consists of those who are not in fellowship or connected with a ministry. George G. Hunter III defines an "apostolic church" as one where the leaders believe that they and the church are "called and sent by God to reach an unchurched pre- Christian population."[82] He discusses various scenarios of people who are not associated with a ministry and how ministry approaches can be designed better to bring these people into fellowship within the body of believers. Hunter stresses that not all unchurched people are in the middle of difficulties or traumatic situations. Ministries must look beyond in order to address not only the brokenness and troubles of people, but to see the areas that are consistently overlooked in order to secure potential opportunities to share as a community of faith. The unchurched are not regular Sunday morning attendees; therefore, they need a reason to connect to the body in order to develop a consistent attendance, as well as an opportunity to grow within the faith.[83]

---

[82] George G. Hunter III, *Church for the Unchurched: The Rebirth of "Apostolic Congregations" across the American Mission Field* (Nashville: Abingdon Press, 1996), 28.

[83] Hunter, 56-58.

Gary L. McIntosh reports that "Hunter prefers to call [the seeker churches] apostolic congregations. Indeed Hunter . . . offered support for seeker services as a reemergence of what churches had always done, target special services toward the nonchurched."[84] The unchurched person's desire is to connect with a cause and with a community of people. Small groups that are relaxed create atmospheres where authenticity is created, and where transparency is developed from person to person. As a result of these settings making a difference in their lives and creating new relationships, the unchurched people invite friends, because they believe that the amount of transformation can assist others similar to themselves in both spiritual formation and development. In reality, the

---

[84] Gary L. McIntosh, "Reaching Secular Peoples: A Review of the Books of George G. Hunter, III," *The Asbury Journal* 66, no. 2 (2011): 114, https://place.asburyseminary.edu/cgi/viewcontent.cgi?referer=https://www.google.com/&httpsredir=1&article=1140&context=asburyjournal (5 February 2021).

unchurched spiritual growth trajectory varies from person to person. Individuals who are classified as the unchurched tend to lean towards acclimating to the church environment through the small group approach that is aligned with discipleship, which prompts continual fellowship experiences. Therefore, in creating these personal settings, leaders must realize that every approach does not render the same effect on every person. Churches must remain cooperative and malleable in their approaches, which allows the individual to pursue self-sufficiency while maintaining connectivity.

Church, as it is known today, has undergone many changes. The cosmetics have shifted and prompted leaders to examine ministry beyond the corporate worship experience and to connect with members on every level. In times past, it has been simple to quantify the "church experience" to the local setting or simply categorize the corporate worship experience as a "one-stop shop." Greg G. Glatz reports:

Bill Hybels founded Willow Creek Community Church in

1975 with the intention of turning "irreligious people into fully devoted followers of Jesus Christ." Willow Creek reinvented worship with live bands, dramas, multimedia accouterments, and accessible theological content in an unconventional meeting space (e.g., Willow Creek Theatre, later replaced by a series of expanding non- traditional structures). Hybels called this a "seeker-sensitive" approach to church.[85]

There are several facets in the church structure that need to be rediscovered such as mission, mandate, and motive. Leaders must structure strategies to build the people, as well as to place people as the priority through letting the gospel become the primary transformation agent. Leaders must actively advance to move towards becoming the tangible representation of the active processes of the gospel that both live and demonstrate the power of liberty among the people.

---

[85] Greg G. Glatz, "2. Getting Past Stalled and Dissatisfied," in *The Great Co- Mission* (n.p.: n.p., 2014), n.p., https://greatcomission.pressbooks.com/chapter/getting-past-stalled-and-dissatisfied/ (5 February 2021).

Ministry innovations have modernized by becoming centered on ways to bring people together on a consistent basis. Ministry features, such as small groups, have afforded leaders within the ministry to become stable fixtures who can be touched and experienced through direct interaction through technology.[86]25 These encounters can give members access to the direct source who can provide unequivocal connections where knowledge and active mentorship can be obtained. Members have that person with whom they can identify on a consistent basis. The settings created by close proximity allow for mutuality, responsibility, and personal progression concurrently under any context. By using the seeker-friendly approach, the leader must go beyond the logistics of the traditional setting in order to find dynamic ministry approaches that meet the needs of the community found within

---

[86] Lynne Hybels and Bill Hybels, *Rediscovering Church: The Story and Vision of Willow Creek Community Church* (Grand Rapids, MI: Zondervan, 1995), 191.

the specific demographics of service. They reinforce the fact that churches can only be effective if they are wholeheartedly in touch with the communities that they serve, while strategically infusing their resources to become agents of improvement, and not exclusive intrusions.

Pastoral leadership is critical to the growth of the church. The role of a pastor carries a set of slated responsibilities that continues to expand as modern-day ministry tackles the difficulties of becoming the church for all people. Pastors are important institutional leaders because they cast vision, and they are the chief servants among those whom they lead. Their leadership can cause a ministry to thrive or to fail, according to their ability to initiate and activate the purpose in others. Stanley E. Jones, Dean C. Barnlund, and Franklyn S. Haiman discuss how the leaders of today must speak the languages of the people and not neglect the place of communication that is most common among the people of today. They also deliberate that there is a prevailing non-Christian culture. Americans live in a society today where Christianity is not popular, and there is a decline within the faith due to paradigm shifts. Pastors cannot readily assume that all others may be like believers. Rather, pastors must face the reality that there is a world of harsh criticism in which they live regularly.[87]

When contrasted with the focus of the current research project, pastors must prepare themselves to deal with the value systems and the callous realities that are faced by people within their communities. Pastoral leaders who are effective must not be passive or slack concerning the precarious issues of governmental institutions and systems. Leadership skills must not only be learned but refined in order to place people strategically to tackle the inconsistencies that are found in their environments. The members of congregations need a measure of strength and consistent structure that does not waiver, but

---

[87] Stanley E. Jones, Dean C. Barnlund, and Franklyn S. Haiman, *The Dynamics of Discussion: Communication in Small Groups*, 2nd ed. (New York: HarperCollins, 1980), 22.

that supports the furtherance of the body of Christ in spiritual health.

Pamela S. Lewis, Stephen H. Goodman, Patricia M. Fandt, and Joseph F. Michlitsch urge that church leaders must be enhanced leaders in more demanding times.[88]

Community is created within the church through both in-reach and outreach. The church's job is to connect with people to increase interest, spawn expansion, and increase the scope of addressing issues that members of congregations deal with throughout their lives. Community is comprised of people. Therefore, the small groups should be structured to address various topics that are mainstream within the community that are stifling the development of those who reside there. Thomas G. Kirkpatrick discusses how the concept of the small groups has infiltrated congregational interactions by creating

---

[88] Pamela S. Lewis, Stephen H. Goodman, Patricia M. Fandt, and Joseph F. Michlitsch, *Management: Challenges for Tomorrow's Leaders*, 4th ed. (Mason, OH: Thomson Learning, 2004), 400.

interconnected networks that assist Christians in sharpening each other. These small groups increase members' transformational effectiveness while providing direction. The current model of traditional churches is becoming obsolete and congregants need a component to address their lives from a holistic perspective.[89]

The 21st century church must contemplate, as well as discern, the undercurrents through which its individual communities flow. Edgar Machel relates:

Besides the quest to create a realistic role description for pastors, the question arises. What kind of personality is needed to deal with the pressures and demands of ministry, not just to survive personally, but to lead a congregation with a positive attitude towards growth? . . . These contextual changes have impacted all churches and the discussions are similar in all denominations. Pastors more than ever are challenged to lead, but traditional pastoral training includes little focus on leadership and church growth.[90]

---

[89] Kirkpatrick, 33-37.

[90] Edgar Machel, "The Relationship Between Leadership

Members of today's churches desire to be part of a faith community where people are transparent, leadership is progressive, and change is visible among the people. There must be a genuine effort to pursue an intentional duty that serves people through serving the Lord. Small groups assist the church in overcoming apparent obstacles that prevent ministry from taking place within the confines of unity. Leaders' authenticity in the community of believers is paramount to the intentionality of the development of the members of the congregation. Small group settings provide safe spaces for people to express themselves in truth, while being unashamed of their vulnerability. Relationships are essential to the sustainability of growth and nurturing among people. To have an authentic group of people also means being

---

Traits and Church Growth Among Pastors of Free Churches in Germany" (Ph.D. diss., Andrews University, 2006), 2-3, https://digitalcommons.andrews.edu/cgi/viewcontent.cgi?article=1545& context=dissertations (5 February 2021).

part of a group where relationships are primary. Activities that help construct those associations among members well past the superficial take the ideals of ministry within the community to transform not the institution, but the outcome among the people.

Church growth occurs outwardly and inwardly through dedicated people who strive to commit to something that is greater than themselves. Growth, within the context of the local assembly, allows people to identify with a small group of people through consistent fostering in all-inclusive areas that assist in the betterment of their lives. Small groups are helpful in that they prompt people to develop in communication, connection, and cause. Church growth should be the strategic crucial point for every ministry. It is the mandate of Christ to spread the gospel to all the ends of the earth. Ronald J. Lavin expresses the importance of experiencing dynamic groups that are small, while growing ministry outwardly. These small groups have been shown to create and identify leaders, as well as their abilities. Through these assemblies of people in close settings, connections are established to give orientation to people beyond the brand of the ministry. Such connections guide them to areas where people can experience true growth in areas that might be deficient or underdeveloped. These groups are rooted in the foundations of fellowship, and now have become part of the fabric of people's daily interactions.[91] Lavin argues that "We either grow or we die. We cannot stay in the same spiritual state. Nothing remains static. It's a law of nature. . . . When I say that your church can grow through small groups, I mean it can grow spiritually through fellowship with Christ and fellow Christians in missions."[92] Small groups are necessary, and Lavin counters the idea that churches do not need them. Rather, churches must focus on the small group

---

[91] Ronald J. Lavin, *Way to Grow! Dynamic Church Growth through Small Groups*
(Lima, OH: CSS Publishing, 1996), 16.

[92] Lavin, 17-18.

approach in order to reach the ever-expanding categories of members whom they serve. Research within Lavin's book says that small groups are not invasive, but are an occasion to build solid connections that directly engage the participants. All of the people who are involved in a church also should be plugged in to a small group, no matter what structure it takes, as a result of each ministry's structure.[93] There are some churches that are based on the traditional model, but that are moving towards small groups as an effort to extend ministry offerings. These undertakings have proven to be strenuous endeavors that require planning and commitment. However, they yield positive outcomes that benefit all ages.

Ministry research is a series of reflections that intentionally examines the stature, strength, and depth of ministry efforts. Within the context of ministry, the purpose of research is to provide information on a journey toward self-discovery in the

---

[93] Lavin, 39-44.

life of the believer in union with the cause put forth in the Christian missive. Ministry research prompts those who undertake it to further their understanding of religious principles about mankind's character and vocation, their carnal tendency to waiver, and their redemption, as well as the urgency to recognize these assurances in connection to both the present-day world and views concerning humanity's existence. These measures have led to a rekindling of the theological attempt to discover more. The role of ministry research is a heavy task that unearths the foundations of believers to bring them to a greater understanding.

Integrating small groups into the congregational setting encourages the ideal that small groups should be deliberate and intentional in the directions of their efforts. The church, in order to remain efficient and effective, must adjust any systems that may be obsolete or deficient.[94] Additionally, after

---

[94] Donald A. McGavran and Win Arn, *How to Grow a Church* (Grand Rapids: Gospel Light, 1973), 162.

discovering weaknesses and deficiencies, solutions can be appropriated to build functions in places that will prompt change, while establishing systematic solidarity. Collaboration is an activity through which people commit to a social situation and develop an essential understanding to make it better for those who will become part of it. Leaders, specifically in ministry, must have a vision and a plan.[95] The success of their ministries is predicated on having qualified leaders who are prepared to carry out the initiatives set forth to provide services to all people. A person has to remain committed to the vision set by the leader, as well as welcome any changes that come with growth. Not only must the leaders embrace change, but the congregants must be willing to support the progressive movement. In order for a church to grow, the people must be connected to their pastor, and vice

---

[95] Loughlan Sofield and Carroll Juliano, *Collaboration: Uniting Our Gifts in Ministry* (Notre Dame, IN: Ave Maria Press, 2000).

versa. There must be a relationship of mutual trust, support, and modernization in order to create a community that benefits all parties who seek to be a part. Members need to understand that the pastor is a chief servant, and his reach is extended by those leaders who serve under him with integrity. The people must understand that leadership, in any capacity, is shared with the congregation and does not belong to just one person. This requires maturity on the part of the believer.[96]

The current project agrees with the perception that church growth, in its entirety, is the responsibility of all people working together. Small groups, which are microcosms of the larger cause, have a way of developing people in environments that are strategically placed. Through these relationships, all people grow in their niches, while growing together at the same time. These ideals are important to substantiate the call

---

[96] Donald P. Smith, *Empowering Ministry: Ways to Grow in Effectiveness*
(Louisville: Westminster John Knox, 1996), 39.

for further investment in the benefit of small groups to churches of all sizes. In understanding the great call that lies on the church, members become more aware of the fact that the work is easily accomplished through the breakdown of plans, while addressing critical issues that affect the people in a simultaneous manner.

The job of the church is to evangelize and to equip believers to go abroad. The tasks are to make new disciples and to grow them into the places where they will be most effective. Glen Martin and Gary McIntosh convey that all people in the community of believers have a designated responsibility to develop the undeveloped and to bring out the best in people.[97] McIntosh presents Bob Morrison's insights that "For most congregations, church size is more important than denominational label in planning for ministry and mission. . . . The leaders of a congregation looking to learn from the

---

[97] Martin and McIntosh, 29.

experiences of others will usually will find it helpful to look at congregations of the same size, regardless of affiliation, rather than limit themselves to churches in the same denomination or association."[98] As leaders make the move forward, they must understand that leadership transitions fluidly with the call or need. The leadership must become synchronized through collaboration, as well as maintain movement so that the leaders do not restrict growth by becoming hindrances.[99] Given the responsibility of the small group in today's church world, it is important that ministries understand the value of small groups in providing a measure of discipleship that pushes people forward.

Small groups are mobilizers for ministry. Senior leadership

---

[98] Gary L. McIntosh, *One Size Doesn't Fit All: Bringing out the Best in Any Size Church* (Grand Rapids: Fleming H. Revell, 1999), 20.

[99] Christopher Novak, *Conquering Adversity: Six Strategies to Move You and Your Team through Tough Times* (Dallas: CornerStone Leadership Institute, 2004), 66.

must understand both position and influence in making small groups appealing to congregational participants through their full support. Members of the congregation are charged to integrate in communal and socialized settings in order to change the lives of the people whom they are called to impact. These settings may differ from the spaces that are considered the norm for church-related fellowship. The conversions obtained from these small-group experiences should reproduce another series of leaders and members who will continue to carry out the instructions that are rooted in discipleship. After the members have been mobilized for growth, they must be charged with both recognizing and using their gifts for the benefit of the body of Christ. Each individual's gift reveals itself to meet the need of another individual who comes through the doors. The communal inclusion that is created by small groups works through posturing any ministry to empower people from diverse backgrounds. Therefore, the congregation takes on direct responsibility to harness people's abilities in order to support the momentum of the ministry substantially, without second-guessing. By doing this, the outlook on change becomes consistent with the vision to win souls, and not just to leave people in the same place where they were found.

Small groups have become the active strategy used in ministry that accelerates the church into a mode that creates bridges for people to establish themselves as part of a collective movement and community. These groups are small imprints that leave lasting impacts on the lives of participants by improving the quality of their lives going forward. The 21st century church has extended its focus by shifting from the preservation of the institution to making people the central focus. The act of building people contributes to the quality of ministry as a whole by giving people the abilities to help local communities improve through positive influences. These groups strategically align people with purpose, and the groups bring people into a place of understanding that they may never have known before.

Reproduction and the revival of "people-centered" hubs are where the needs of a person become a concern for the consciousness of the people. This consciousness pushes people to act and to make change for the better. By doing this, the expediters make space for the community to place communal concerns in a position of priority. McIntosh gives Morrison's view: "In the small church, the organizational principle is *relational orientation*. Another way to describe it is familial orientation. One needs to think of the small church as a large extended family."[100] Churches must refuse to make this a secondary thought, and must allow it to become one of the most important facets of the church's culture. Small groups are the building blocks of large congregations and are key to the furtherance of ministry. The diversities found within these groups are needed to build unique structures that will change

---

[100] McIntosh, *One Size Doesn't Fit All*, 27.

the lives of people holistically and will provide a refuge for those who are unprotected against the inequalities found within society.

Gareth Weldon Icenogle discusses scriptural foundations that are related to small groups and the necessity of fellowship as believers. "Covenant" is the term used by God to define relationship. "It is God's 'unilateral' word and action."[101] The church has decreased its attention towards specific issues within the communal setting that have restrained effective discipleship and neutralized authentic community without judgement.

The small group has become a connecting point in the relationship between the church and the congregant. Small groups include mentorship components that help shape the lives of people of all ages through intentional guidance and

---

[101] Gareth Weldon Icenogle, *Biblical Foundations for Small Group Ministry: An Integrational Approach* (Downers Grove, IL: InterVarsity Press, 1994), 37.

extended accountability in completing endeavors outside the church environment. The small group encompasses well-defined restructured openings for members to participate in shared fellowship, in faith-related involvement, to collect information, and to flourish together.

Icenogle's ministry approach informs the current research that all groups must demonstrate biblical principles that are grounded in fellowship. The nature of Jesus' model for discipleship proved to be successful as he developed twelve men and walked alongside them for a purpose.[102] Ministry groups must meet people and understand them in order to grow them effectively. Small groups should structure themselves according to the needs of the people. The organizational structures of churches are different than those of other mainstream social contexts. Systematically viewed as a hierarchical structure of power relationships, it is of highest

---

[102] Icenogle, 119-125.

priority that the practical issues regarding these relationships need to be addressed in order to create a culture where everyone is significant and where no one is excluded.

The small group has shown itself to be a central influence in providing a foundation for extensive church growth via discipleship through constantly making connectivity available that includes numerous resources for groups members to lead effective lives. Although the small group is a communal platform used within discipleship, it is designed primarily to deliver a measure of congregational care and oversight to members while offering an opportunity for them to become intricate parts of the faith community. Personal discovery happens in small groups better than in large groups for a number of reasons. One can acquire information, ask questions without judgment, include oneself in the lives of others, and come to know other people who are doing the same things in small groups. Corporate worship experiences do not carry the same weight. Spiritual growth happens better in conjunction with others in community, and with communication and liberty to speak life into another individual.

Missions can be planned out and participated in together in integrated environments where collaboration is celebrated, lives are improved, and leaders established. Small groups are a requirement for involving as many people as possible in the life and ministry of the church. Mark A. Lamport and Mary Rynsburger stipulate:

> Awareness of the internal and external forces affecting any group—including a small church group—is important for the leader to act in a way to help accomplish the goal of the group. . . . While identifying the forces affecting each individual seems impossible, such forces exert a considerable effect on a person's perception of the material being studied, on what is communicated by others in the group, and on a person's potential for life application.[103]

Small groups are extensive platforms through which teaching

---

[103] Mark A. Lamport and Mary Rynsburger, "All the Rage: How Small Groups are Really Educating Christian Adults; Part 2: Augmenting Small Group Ministry Practice—Developing Small Group Leadership Skills through Insights from Cognate Theoretical Disciplines," *Christian Education Journal* 5, no. 2 (2008): 392. 391-414.

can take on a greater transformative role within a localized body Small groups are entities that actually supplement these structural variations by making available a support for congregants and pastors to define balanced, two-way positions. Through this channel, an archetype is developed to empower people meaningfully to take over in roles of leadership and responsibility. The church becomes an organism that develops, matures, and grows into maturity, while doing the same in people's lives.

Ministry innovations, such as small groups, have allowed ministry leaders to become visible through dependable interfaces where personal development can take place. A small group ministry that thrives is built on a circle of reciprocity that continually gives the best of itself to build. The small group is the essential element that builds the ideals of community within the church, because there is always a new influx of people who are seeking to connect. Small groups work well in a congregational setting by being consciously transformative. Change is an essential component of discipleship, and change is a fundamental constituent of congregational life in vibrant shared communities. A place of apprehension felt by all churches is in sustaining the uprightness of their theological principles while being accommodating in the approaches by which they allocate and exercise those beliefs. In many churches, introducing and enabling change in practice, such as with small groups, is challenging. [104] However, skilled leadership with an understanding of community provides a method to employ considerable organizational variations through united contemplation and discussion. The development of community, authorizing quality of small groups, gives the participants a place of input and a say in the process of making decisions and implementing changes to group operations.

---

[104] C. J. Mahaney, "Why Small Groups?" in *Why Small Groups?* ed. C. J. Mahaney (Gaithersburg, MD: Sovereign Grace Ministries, 1996), 11.

Change is not executed by leadership alone, but through relationship and compromise.[105]

Small groups step into communities in ways that are informal, understandable, and considered. Building thriving small groups requires putting both the best resources and energy into an infrastructure that can handle break-out and progressive change.[106] The goal is to build widespread community by design that leaves no room for people to remain disconnected. Vision should be cast among the community of faith in such a way that it is visible for the leaders.

According to Lazarus Ndiku Makewa et al., "Frustration is one of the most commonly mentioned negative emotions

---

[105] 44Greg Somerville, "Take This Group and Own It!" in *Why Small Groups?* ed. C.
J. Mahaney (Gaithersburg, MD: Sovereign Grace Ministries, 1996), 36.

[106] Mary B. McRae, Patricia M. Carey, and Roxanna Anderson-Scott, "Black Churches as Therapeutic Systems: A Group Process Perspective," *Health Education & Behavior* 25, no. 6 (1998): 778-789.

associated with group learning. . . . Some collaborative learning environments may interfere with students' willingness to engage in the project. They may also experience stress and frustration in collaborating with people they do not know well."[107] The same can be said for small groups in the ministry setting. There are frustrations for leadership within the church because the communities that they are in may take on a different context. There may be layered issues, social obstacles, economic barriers, and practices within the community that may be contrary to the communal work that is being attempted. However, resistance should not completely deter the work; rather, resistance should serve as a catalyst to become proactive in all things that the community seeks to do in order to become an asset to the demographics that the

---

[107] Lazarus Ndiku Makewa et al., "Frustration Factor in Group Collaborative Learning Experiences," *American Journal of Educational Research* 2, no. 11A (2014): 18, https://www.researchgate.net/publication/269334783_Frustration_Factor_in_Group_Collaborative_Learning_Experiences (5 February 2021).

ministry is assigned to serve. This project proposes the idea that encouragement in action through the small-group platform will afford chances to garner collaboration and empowerment that fit with Christian obligations to the betterment of all people, regardless of gender, ethnicity, and social equality.

Most Notable Small Group Model

The Purpose-Driven small groups model, developed from Rick Warren's experiences at Saddleback Church, are noted in his book *The Purpose-Driven Church*. "Each innovation we've developed was just a *response* to the circumstances in which we found ourselves. I didn't plan them in advance. Most people think of "vision" as the ability to see the future. But in today's rapidly changing world, vision is also the ability to accurately assess current changes and take advantage of them. Vision is being alert to opportunities"[108] This model seeks intentionally to deepen five areas in each small group: fellowship, discipleship, ministry, evangelism, and worship.[109] This model does not emphasize duplication as a system to expand the ministry but depends instead on regular church-

---

[108] Rick Warren, *The Purpose-Driven Church* (Grand Rapids: Zondervan, 1995), 28.

[109] Warren, *The Purpose-Driven Church*, 143.

wide movements. Within these crusades, new leaders are primarily enlisted as presenters, and then they are prepared as spiritual front-runners over the course of time.

The advantage of this type of ministry group is that it focuses on five purposes that convey the capability for more active and involved disciples of Jesus Christ. Training new leaders as presenters decreases the level of anticipation by making more potential leaders accessible. Growth through campaigns permits individual groups to increase trust and intimacy without being anxious about an ultimate breakup.

There are four types of small groups commonly used in present-day ministries. These groups afford congregants the opportunity to be involved extensively within the life of the congregation on the basis of their individual life needs. Each of these groups is designed with the intention of developing the member holistically in the areas for which they express need. Warren explains, "Some involve group members for ministry. Some help church members develop a relationship with non-Christians—and others try to help believers deal with the overwhelming crises of life. Yet all of them have one thing in common—they connect people with others at the church. Each is connected to a different purpose of the church."[110] The four types of groups are membership, maturity, ministry, and missions.

The following is a brief summary of each type:

- Membership: These groups focus on the crises of life—addictions, victimizations, terminal illness, etc. These are our care groups and Celebrate Recovery groups.
- Maturity: These are what most people think of when they think of small groups. Our maturity groups focus on all the purposes—worship, fellowship, discipleship, ministry, and evangelism. They meet in homes and study a biblical topic or a book of the Bible.
- Ministry: These groups are built around ministries in the church. You may not think of them as small groups, but they are. Your ushers are in a group. Your music ministry is a group. Your greeters are a group. They are not only serving the church, but they're building relationships in the group. These relationships make your

---

[110] Rick Warren, "Small Groups: 4 Kinds that Expand Ministry," *Pastors.com*, 1 October 2012, n.p., https://pastors.com/small-groups-4-kinds-that-expand-ministry/ (6 February 2021).

church feel smaller.

- Missions: The whole focus of these groups is reaching people who are not Christians. These are what we used to call "seeker" Bible studies. They allow people who have questions about the Bible to come and explore it in a safe environment. They could be outreach Bible studies held in local businesses.

They could be mission teams that do not meet together to study anything; they meet to do missions together. Nothing ties a group of people together better than a common purpose, particularly when that purpose is reaching people with the gospel.[111]

Our sanity and survival depended upon developing a workable process to turn seekers into saints, turn consumers into contributors, turn members into ministers, and turn an audience into an army. Believe me, it is an incredibly difficult task to lead people from self-centered consumerism to being servant-hearted Christians. It is not a task for fainthearted ministers or those who don't like to get their religious robes

---

[111] Warren, "Small Groups: 4 Kinds that Expand Ministry," n.p.

wrinkled. But it *is* what the Great Commission is all about and it has been the driving force behind all that has happened so far at Saddleback.[112]

These groups are being executed at Warren's Saddleback Church. Saddleback Church is one of America's largest and most influential churches. Warren was born in San Jose, California. He holds "a Bachelor of Arts from California Baptist University, a Master of Divinity from Southwestern Theological Seminary, and a Doctor of Ministry from Fuller Theological Seminary." Saddleback Church was founded when Warren was only 26 years old. He has moved this vision forward, and presently he serves as its Senior Pastor.[113]

Saddleback is a purpose-driven church that extends into the field of active ministry through evangelism, fellowship, ministry, discipleship, and worship. Saddleback began as a

---

[112] Warren, *The Purpose-Driven Church*, 46.

[113] Saddleback Church, "Our Pastor," *Saddleback.com*, n.d., n.p., https:// saddleback.com/visit/about/pastors/our-pastor (5 January 2021).

church plant thirty-five years ago The model was based on attracting people who would not normally frequent traditional worship settings, along with those people who refused to attend church altogether. The beginnings of the ministry are rooted, specifically, in small group Bible study. The church held its first worship service with 205 people in 1980.[114]

At present, Saddleback Church has many locations. In *The Purpose Driven Church.*, Warren outlines the effective principles that contributed to the ministry's expansion, growth, and continued success. Rick Warren explains that these are "the result of balancing the five biblical purposes of the church—Worship, Fellowship, Discipleship, Ministry, and Mission." [115] The small groups are able to be chosen by prospective members based on their preferences. To align with

---

[114] Saddleback Church, "Our Church," *Saddleback.com*, n.d., n.p., https:// saddleback.com/visit/about/our-church (5 January 2021).

[115] Rick Warren, "Twelve Characteristics of a Purpose Driven Church," *Pd.church*, n.d., n.p., https://pd.church/12-characteristics-purpose-driven-church/ (12 January 2021).

a specific group, the potential member fills out a demographic form that links them directly with their location, meeting days, age group, gender, life stage, and language.[116]

The membership group provides an opportunity for people to connect with each other as they engage the Word in an applicable way to develop in their normal, everyday lives. In the maturity group, discipleship and study are key priorities. Believers seek to learn from each other with interconnected environments that lead to acquisition of biblical principles in a practical way. These groups give congregants the ability to question scripture, to dialogue, and to interact in a face-to-face approach. These groups assist in developing a diverse perspective through the eyes of believers who come from different backgrounds. In the study component, church members learn to understand the Bible and their relationship to scripture as individuals. They are bonded through

---

[116] Rick Warren, *40 Days of Community Study Guide* (Grand Rapids: Zondervan, 2012), 44.

communal interaction and collective accountability to the word of God. The combination of a capable Bible teacher and eager learners who are exchanging ideas together can become a transformational experience.[117]

The ministry group model for small groups is designed around either specific tasks or defined purposes found within the Saddleback Church construct. Small groups of this type are responsible for strengthening the core of the church and the personnel who function in various ministries. In these group settings are professional development and leadership engagement opportunities to train individuals on core topics that affect their functionality in the local ministry setting. These programs are intentionally blended because of the varying dynamics of the ministry, including physical churches, extended campuses, and online ministry connections. These

---

[117] Nelus Niemandt, *Missional Leadership*, HTS Religion and Society Series, vol. 7 (Cape Town, SA: AOSIS, 2019), 13-14.

programs are guided, paced, and regimented. They bring participants together face-to-face, or they deliver learning where there is a need for resources, people, and equipment to which they may not have access in their local setting.[118]

The missions group is focused on reaching those who are within its geographical area, or internationally. Based on the convictions of a given ministry, the goal of these groups is to extend ministry services and personnel to populations that might be underserved or even forgotten. The heartbeat of this small group ministry approach is to keep the needs of the community and the world at the forefront. This type of group exists to reinforce the Great Commission and to develop missions leaders who see missions as a global ministry that prepares them for success in diversified environments and overseas missions.[119]

---

[118] Paul Borthwick, *New Directions for Small-Group Ministry* (Loveland, CO: Vital Ministry, 1999), 101-102.

[119] Denny Spitters and Mathew Ellison, *When Everything is Missions* (Orlando, FL: BottomLine Media, 2017), 48.

The 40-Day Campaign Strategy

Warren reports, "Our first membership class drew twenty people. Eighteen of them were unbelievers, so I had to begin by teaching the most elementary truths of the Christian life. By the end of the six-week class, all eighteen unbelievers had accepted Christ, were baptized, and were welcomed into membership."[120] This small group method is one noted for easy accessibility. Comprised of a six-week timeline, these groups are part of a church-wide campaign. The studies that take place within these groups are intentionally connected as a reinforcement of the sermon, while the entire church is on the same page. Rather than have typical group leaders, there are hosts who are facilitators in these settings. The goal is to have participants commit and then continue afterward.

---

[120] Warren, *The Purpose-Driven Church*, 44.

The Mid-Sized Geographic Strategy

Warren explains, "The first task of leadership is to define the mission, so I tried to paint, in attractive terms, the picture as clearly as I saw it. Over the years we've returned again and again to that vision statement for midcourse corrections. Our vision has never really focused on getting big or erecting buildings; instead, our vision has been to produce disciples of Jesus Christ." [121] This group model takes an on-going approach.

However, it differs in two specific ways. First, the groups are organized by geographic areas. The reason for this placement is because the community development is linked to the premise that people live in the same area as one another; therefore, the community will develop. Second, the groups, when connected, form groups of a large size. As a result, socialization and the mission of the ministry is advanced within the larger community. These groups are location-based.

---

[121] Warren, *The Purpose-Driven Church*, 42.

Cell-Based Church

Warren declares:

I've learned that most people can't hear until they've first been heard. People don't care how much we know until they know how much we care. Intelligent, caring conversation opens the door for evangelism with nonbelievers faster than anything else I've used. It is *not* the church's task to give people whatever they want or even need. But the fastest way to build a bridge to the unchurched is to express interest in them and show that you understand the problems they are facing.[122]

The model for the cell church differs from the other models because the church is comprised of cell groups. Participation by the congregants is done through each individual cell. The cell group carries the ability to grow, and the ultimate push is for the group to multiply in number. This model is a continuation of the open-group strategy.

The only distinction is that the cell group is an only a part of the larger church, and not the church itself. The cell group is at the micro-level. The church is the macro-level.

Although the difference is small, the impact is big.

---

[122] Warren, *The Purpose-Driven Church*, 40.

Missional Communities

Warren explains, "As we saw God confirm our decision to begin the church in many, many ways in those early days, we learned an important lesson: *Wherever God guides, he provides.*"[123] The group takes on many appearances, but it is rooted in accomplishing a set mission. As many as two or three groups can merge. The characteristic that sets apart this group model is that the community is the center of activity that drives both efforts and decisions. It is the community that takes on the concept of kingdom culture to bring ministry into a specific area or neighborhood.

Small Group Research Strategy

Human beings are relational beings. Therefore, they are not designed to live alone or to be isolated from community. Disciples of Jesus Christ, with connections to congregational community, are cultivated through the local church. They are

---

[123] Warren, *The Purpose-Driven Church*, 38.

enriched in both personhood and purpose through interconnected relationships with other individuals who partake in daily congregational life. These people can be like-minded or can have diverse perspectives, which reveal the essential nature of human development in relationships.

Small groups are a congregational strategy used to foster intentional close relationships with each other. These groups are transformative, because they form communities of accountability, coupled with authentic support for daily life with Christ at the center. Small groups are critical to discipleship as they provide interconnected opportunities for people to create safe places for shared experiences. A small group is where people love, forgive, serve, carry each other's burdens, encourage, pray, speak of truth, confess, and treat each other with love and respect. As a result, this environment becomes a catalyst for spiritual formation and subsequently reinforces the purpose of the church. Julie Gorman explains, "True community is more than being together. A person does

not develop trust in others by simply being in a group where members study together, pray together, and share a common group leader. Trust involves relatedness. Relatedness is more than presence although it is the beginning. To relate, one must know, and to know one must work at being open to trust."[124]
A small group can be comprised of three to fifteen people who meet regularly (weekly, biweekly, or monthly) to help one another grow in holiness of heart and life, and to equip the congregation to participate in God's mission in the world. Group members attend to the ways that God is at work in their lives, and they do all in their power to help one another grow in faith, hope, and love.

Given the vital role of the small groups in today's church world, this study examined the value of the use of small groups

---

[124] Julie Gorman, *Community That is Christian* (Colorado Springs: Chariot Victor, 1993), 98; quoted in Bill Donahue and Russ Robinson, *Building a Church of Small Groups: A Place Where Nobody Stands Alone* (Grand Rapids: Zondervan, 2001), 60, n. 3.

in local church settings with specific references to perspectives and the role that they play in inspiring a transformative move in their usage in the development of disciples. This study was significant because it involved exploring the acceptability of (attitudes toward) small groups as a useful factor in increasing the effectiveness and transformational shifting of their current practices as found in a discipleship model.

The purpose of this study was to determine the success of small groups used as a platform within a discipleship model within the 21st century church. This study also sought to determine the success of executing small groups in a church environment through establishing a pilot model to enhance the reach of individual attention and interest for the congregation as well as the community. The perceptions of church leaders about the use of small groups as a discipleship strategy are a concern, as well as its integration into the mainstream of the church discipleship model. Through this study, the significant impact of the small groups was seen in a designated series of small group environments, and documented to prove the critical character of their presence within the discipleship model through expanding the church's reach and personal development practice in the local ministry setting.

The provisions of this study will generate an opportunity to access the distinctive influences of the small group in regard to the personal development of congregants and the creation of new ideas and innovative practices regarding creating authentic faith communities within the church through discipleship. Provisions will also establish a point of access to approach the exclusive influences of small groups in regard to the development of an effective model of discipleship in the 21st century church. By examining the sequence of events and the engagement with this discipleship tool, a clearer point of view was obtained regarding development measures within people and subsequent small group offerings to ensure the maximum reassurance level with the use of small groups, as well as its proper integration into the discipleship model. The project will contribute greatly to the construction of new ideas and ministerial practices within the field of ministry.

Rationale for Methodology

The rationale behind this quantitative study's focus was to determine the effectiveness and progression of the use of small groups to create an effective model of discipleship in the 21st century church. The study gave experienced pastors and emerging ministry leaders a new perspective on how to propel small group offerings and fellowship experiences to a completely new height with endless potential. Small groups are among the current ministry practices that are characterized by their intricate methods for forming community, fostering authentic connectivity, and substantiating their validity in the dynamic of congregational life. The study served to set a foundation for expanding future community and congregational ministry goals, intentional programming, and ministry standards. Through execution of the research, the researcher provided a measure for assessing the individuals who participated, as well as the nature of participants' perceptions. The goal was to construct the research in such a way that it defined, clarified, and projected.

Nature of the Research Design for the Study

This study was designed to investigate specific hypotheses, to survey cause-and-effect, and to make related subsequent projections. The participants were selected randomly in order to study specific variables. The quantitative data particular to this specific design was based on precise measurements using structured and validated data- collection instruments. The identification of statistical relationships was essential, while objectivity remained critical. The researcher's biases were not known to participants within the study. The participants' characteristics were deliberately concealed from the researcher. The research inquiry produced findings that are generalizable and that can be applied to other populations. The structure took on an acquiescent or top-down strategy, where the researcher tested the hypothesis and theory with the data.

The study granted a distinct perspective from a narrow-angle lens, and allowed the opportunity to test specific hypotheses. The structure of this research investigation allowed review of behaviors under controlled conditions, and isolated causal effects. Considering this factor, the nature of reality was that of a single reality combined with the concentration of objectivity. The statistical report will be presented with connections, the comparisons of averages, and the statistical significance of outcomes.

Participants

There were approximately 200 small group participants who lived in a southern metropolitan city. Small group participants ranged in age from 20 years to 65 or more years. The sample of participants was solicited from the Consolidated Metropolitan Full Gospel Baptist Church (CMFGBC). The pool for the participants varied from general membership to non-members who fellowshipped within the small group ministry setting. This ministry entity was a Full-Gospel Baptist

Church established and redeveloped within the past ten years. The research site was assigned an acronym that represented the actual church; thus, the acronym was used to protect the privacy of the institutions (per the policy agreed upon when receiving approval to conduct the study).

CMFGBC was founded in the summer of 2011. On March 24, 1992, the Bishop and six members met to organize CMFGBC. Originally, the church began with prayer service and Bible study in the home of a deacon and deaconess in Bossier City, Louisiana. In this modest beginning, the church committed to the Great Commission of the Lord to evangelize and win the lost at all costs. In April of 1992, the church was incorporated as a non-profit organization. On Sunday, April 19, 1992, the church held its first worship service in Shreveport, Louisiana. The membership immediately grew from seven to 30 members. The church remained at this location until September, 1992, when the church moved. During its second year of existence, CMFGBC became known as the "Church where the doors swing on the hinges of love." CMFGBC also coined the descriptive phrases "Spiritual Hospital" and "House of Refuge" due to the heightened care and concern for God's people. In September, 1993, the growth of CMFGBC accelerated beyond its physical capacity.

In October, 1993, the church moved to a storefront. Once again, growth accelerated tremendously to approximately 200 members. On Easter Sunday, 1996, CMFGBC formed a motorcade and entered the current location in Shreveport, Louisiana. The dedication of CMFGBC to Bishop Paul S. Morton and the Full Gospel Baptist Church Fellowship was so vast that in May, 1997, the name of the church was officially changed to the Consolidated Metropolitan Full Gospel Baptist Church. On Easter Sunday, 1997, CMFGBC expanded their current ministry and branched out, thereby making them known as "one church in two cities." At the time of this study, CMFGBC had more than 900 members on record, including 10 pastoring sons and daughters.

CMFGBC is currently associated with the Full Gospel Baptist Church Fellowship. The ministry is affiliated with the Home Mission Board of the Southern Baptist Convention and the American Baptist Churches of USA. CMFGBC also was affiliated with the Unity Celebration Fellowship.

The ministry centered its philosophy on creating environments that promoted the development of fellowship through intentional practices of growth reflected through communal learning. The participants within this study consisted of all participants of the small (cell) groups at CMFGBC. The participants were recruited on the grounds that they were active small (cell) group members. Additionally, they were recruited because there had been a recent period when considerable efforts were made towards small group development.

Circumstances for Research

Although ministry formats have changed, small groups have created a space of debate in regard to the organizational structure of ministry dynamics. The circumstances surrounding small groups have caused discontent, which has led to stress for ministry leaders in their attempts to accommodate the ever-expanding needs of growing congregations while managing a stable ministry dynamic. Therefore, many ministry leaders have become careful, divergent, and disregarding of the practice of small groups in their discipleship paradigms and congregational care preparations. This study examined probable stimuli that might provide clarification for the changes and viewpoints regarding how ministries utilize the small group program in their local church settings.

Current research has indicated that churches esteem the small group model as an element with educational and personal value that realizes interconnectivity within their congregations, yet very few churches fully integrate the small group into every feature of church events.[125] Furthermore, it

---

[125] John Mallison, *Building Small Groups in the Christian*

seems that previous research in this area has unsuccessfully surveyed the limited boundaries challenged by distinct discipleship reproductions and the mindsets that are extended as a result of exercising the small group in the church of today.

Research Questions

Three research questions guided this study. Research Question 1 was: Are small (cell) groups effective in addressing the needs of the local church? The first objective was to determine participants' experiences in small (cell) groups in their ministry; therefore, Research Question 2 was: Do the experiences (i.e. connectional activities and teachings) within the small (cell) groups address the needs of the local church? The second objective was to determine the progress of increased participation in ministry aspects and how accurately this predicts small cell groups' progress; therefore, Research

---

Community (West Ryde, NSW: Renewal Publications, 1979), 6.

Question 3 was: Have ministry aspects (i.e., tithes and offerings, church attendance, volunteer population, fellowship attendance during special events, altar calls, cell group attendance, cell group leaders, and baptism participants) increased or decreased since small (cell) groups have been established within the ministry?

Procedures

The researcher received approval from the Oral Roberts University Institutional Review Board (IRB) to conduct the study. The researcher received approval from CMFGBC, as well as its administration, to conduct and oversee the research at the site. Bishop Lawrence Brandon, who was the Third Presiding Bishop of the Full Gospel Baptist Church Fellowship, International, and was the researcher, arranged for the survey to be disseminated at a designated time in a designated room located at the respective site through the administrator. Therefore, there was ministry-wide distribution and administration of the instrument to CMFGBC, which made this site specifically unique.

The focus of the study was to provide direct answers to the questions of "how" and "why" in regard to small cell group participants and their perspectives towards the effectiveness and progress of the congregation. The researcher could not manipulate the behaviors or the responses of those who were involved in the study. The conditions within the context were covered because they were relevant to the phenomenon that was studied. The researcher contacted the administrator of CMFGBC in order to seek clearance to facilitate the use of a Research Survey (with Participant Demographics and Survey Instrument). This Research Survey was used to provide the essential measurements of the dependent variables.

The Research Survey was administered on a specified date that was determined by the researcher. The participants were instructed to complete the survey on a voluntary basis. The administrator of CMFGBC provided the survey to the leadership. The participants read a brief description that explained the study and the research parameters. After they had obtained a general knowledge of the study, they signed the Survey Consent Form (Appendix A). Once the informed consent was signed, the participants placed the consent forms in an envelope designated for all consent forms.

Because the Participant Demographics were included in the whole Research Survey (Appendix B), this began the process of completing the survey entitled "The Success of Small Groups as a Discipleship Model in the 21st Century Church."

Completion of the Research Survey, which included the Participant Demographics and the Survey Instrument, was expected to take approximately 15 minutes. Participants submitted the completed surveys on computer via Qualtrics XM software. (No hard copy/print surveys were administered). All participants were sent an anonymous survey link with a designated number for the purpose of identification. The raw data was recorded in the Qualtrics secure servers. The software ensured that relevant data were collected, by organizing and collecting important metrics that were relative to each participant's experience in small discipleship groups. This included making sure that the right question types were both selected and crafted to answer the proposed research questions adequately. Bias was avoided in the survey by refraining from providing information that disclosed what the researcher wanted the study to show. The researcher employed structural designs to avoid survey respondent fatigue or failure to complete.

Prior to administration, the survey was tested within the Qualtrics system to ensure that it ran smoothly, that questions were easy to understand, and that design details like mobile-optimization worked as intended. Once the researcher acted on feedback from the testing stage, he was able to launch the survey across multiple channels confidently. Qualtrics XM instantly recorded the data upon the completion of each survey.[126]

---

[126] Jennifer E. Cushman, Miriah Russo Kelly, Maryann

Utilizing this software helped the researcher generate a better understanding of any changes that needed to be made, and to act accordingly. The researcher was able to understand the participants' wants, needs, pain-points, common issues, and high points. From this, content could be created that ensured the researcher was focused on the specific research population. Ultimately, after administration of the survey, the researcher received feedback based on his points of inquiry, based on key demographics that were specific to this research.

All research materials were assigned a confidential number for coding purposes; anonymity was promised. In addition, confidential survey responses only were released to the researcher and to CMFGBC. Consent forms and survey data were kept in a secure file, identified only by number, and only

---

Fusco-Rollins, and Ryan Faulkner, "Resource Review—Using Qualtrics Core XM for Surveying Youth," *Journal of Youth Development* 16, no. 1 (2021): 161-167. https://jyd.pitt.edu/ojs/jyd/article/view/21-16-1-RR-3/1231 (28 August 2022).

were accessible to the officials of CMFGBC and the researcher. The participants were allowed to choose not to participate or to withdraw at any time during the study. Participants were told that they were free to withhold their responses on the open feedback sections of the survey. On a specified date that was scheduled by the researcher, the survey data were retrieved by the researcher and coded for the purposes of developing visuals for the data.

To eliminate any areas of bias, the investigator, as well as administrators, remained neutral in all questions, no matter how intense the topic. This was implemented in order to ensure that the researcher had a full comprehension of the issue being studied. Additionally, the investigator understood the advantages and disadvantages of each question type that was utilized. This detail was determined by the previous use and implementation of the instrument being evaluated for the intended use of this study.

Therefore, the questions and choices not only were selected

correctly, but were adapted exclusively in order to provide only the most suitable data.

There were no perceived or potential risks to participants involved in this undertaking; therefore, the researcher was responsible for any risks, discomforts, or inconveniences that might have occurred. Ethical considerations were of the highest priority. Human research with any subject can only be conducted upon ethical approval by the necessary channels. The IRB determined the validity of sound ethics via the nature of the standards related to the risks of the research. There was a set of centralized standards that were in place not only for consideration purposes, but to prevent any area of compromise regarding the participation of any human subjects. Attached to these slated standards was the distinction regarding the specific area of research and the reliability regarding the extent of the study that was conducted. The code of ethics that were used with this study were more than the acceptance for these standards. The dispositions ensured and maintained a secure level of mutual confidentiality and foundational trust in the relationship between the researcher and the participants.

Therefore, the highest level of ethical equality and integrity was sustained.

Analysis

The Statistical Package for the Social Sciences (SPSS) was used to perform statistical analyses to test two hypotheses.[127] Hypothesis 1 was: Experiences within the small (cell) groups address the needs of the local church (i.e., fellowship, accountability, leadership development, charity/service work, church member, care and engagement, organization by the leader, message dissemination, impartation of spiritual gifts, increase in church attendance, and intercessory work). Hypothesis 2 was: There will be positive correlation between increased participation in small (cell) groups that have been

---

[127] 4Raynald Levesque and SPSS Inc, *SPSS Programming and Data Management: A Guide for SPSS and SAS Users*, 4th ed. (Chicago: SPSS, Inc., 2007)

established within the ministry and the participant's age.

When analyzing surveys, the researcher's main objective or primary goal was to get the unprocessed data into a form that could be handled. Survey item responses were structured with a Likert scale. Likert scales give quantitative value to qualitative data.

The survey was designed to measure how much each participant agrees/disagrees with a statement, or is satisfied/dissatisfied regarding a specific value related to small groups, and a point value was assigned. The SPSS was used to perform statistical analyses. Raw data were entered into the system. The software automatically collated the data after it was entered. Each question was given a number as a column heading. There was one row for each participant's answers. Then a number or code was assigned to each possible answer. The researcher assessed each participant's questionnaire by adding in the codes.

Once the researcher entered the data from all the surveys into the system, the data were reviewed for accuracy by an outsourced credible statistician. If there were any errors, then the data were reviewed again and corrected. After the data was verified, accounted for, and concluded to be correct, then the number of responses for each item were counted. Once the researcher calculated how many participants selected each response, the researcher developed a series of tables to display the data. After all data analyses had taken place, a narrative summary was developed to interpret the findings in terms of the research questions.

Participant Demographics

The Participant Demographics part of the Research Survey was used to collect each participant's age group, gender, ethnicity, employment status, marital status, and education level, as well as the number of groups attended that emphasized certain topics. The demographic information allowed the researcher to better understand these characteristics of the participants. The demographics helped identify the types of people who comprised the participants who took part in small groups. Collecting this type of information helped the researcher understand the Survey Instrument results better, because different identities and traits can impact small group experiences. Demographics allowed the researcher to examine both the overall results and the meaning among the small group participants at the research site. The demographic information aided in honing in on those local differences—such as age, gender, ethnicity—thereby helping to ensure consistency across the experience.

Description of the Research Survey

The Research Survey consisted of two components. The first part was the Participant Demographics which provided information on the number and types of study participants, as clarified to whom the study findings applied. Additionally, it shed light on the generalizability of the findings, as well as any possible limitations. Accurate reporting was a priority for any replication of the study that might be carried out in the future.

Noteworthy here was that the subject selection in this research study was purposeful— participants were selected who could best inform the research questions and enhance understanding of the phenomenon under study. Thus, the Participant Demographics was an essentially important part in the study design to aid in sufficiently identifying appropriate participants.

The second portion of the Research Survey was the actual Survey Instrument, entitled "The Use of Small Groups to Create an Effective Model of Discipleship in the 21st Century." This was a 19-item survey, with item responses based on a Likert scale. It was a type of psychometric response scale in which responders specified their level of agreement or satisfaction with a statement with five possible responses of two types: (1) Strongly Disagree, (2) Disagree, (3) Neither Agree Nor Disagree, (4) Agree, (5) Strongly Agree; as well as (1) Not At All Satisfied, (2) Slightly Satisfied, (3) Moderately Satisfied, (4) Very Satisfied, (5) Completely Satisfied.

Respondents chose the option that best corresponded with how they felt about the statement. A Likert scale was used in this Research Survey to assess opinions, attitudes, or behaviors. The researcher selected the Likert scale because it allowed for easily operationalizing personality traits or perceptions.

Measures

The demographic information assessed each participant's age, sex, ethnicity, employment, marital status, education, and number of small groups attended that emphasized the any topic of biblical teaching, education, life skills, or personal development. The Survey Instrument contained items that helped in developing a summary of small group participants' dispositions and feelings towards the effectiveness and progress of small cell groups in the ministry setting. This was done with survey items that used a Likert-type scale. Those questions will be scored using a 5-point Likert scale that ranges from 1 = Not at all satisfied to 5 = Completely satisfied, and 1 = Strongly Disagree to 5 = Strongly Agree.

DISCIPLESHIP RESEARCH SURVEY

The Use of Small Groups to Create an Effective Model of Discipleship in the 21st Century Church

The survey will be accessible via Qualtrics XM. The format mentioned, below, contains all questions listed in the survey.

Thank you for taking part in this survey. This survey is intended to recognize your attitudes and experiences with cell groups in the church you are leading. Please answer as truthfully as possible.

Thank you for your time, but I request that you fill out this

survey on or before July 2022.

Sincerely,

Larry Lawrence Brandon

PARTICIPANT PROFILE

1. Age
[ ] 20-25 years [ ] 26-35 years [ ] 36-45 years [ ] 46-55 years
[ ] 65 or more years

2. Sex
[ ] Male
[ ] Female [ ] Intersex

3. Ethnicity [ ] White [ ] Black [ ] Asian
[ ] American Indian/Alaska native [ ] Hawaiian/Pacific Islander
[ ] Mixed Ethnicity

4. Employment [ ] Full-Time [ ] Part-Time
[ ] Unemployed

5. Marital Status [ ] Single
[ ] Married [ ] Divorced
[ ] Widowed

6. Education
[ ] HS Diploma [ ] GED
[ ] Associates Degree (A.A., A.S., etc.)
[ ] Bachelors Degree (B.A., B.S., etc.)
[ ] Masters Degree (M.A., M.S., etc.)
[ ] Doctorate Degree (Ph.D., Ed.D., D.Min., Th.D.)

7. Number of Small Groups Attended that emphasized any topic of biblical teaching, education, life skills, or personal development.
[ ] 1
[ ] 2
[ ] 3
[ ] 4 or More

RESULTS OF THE DISCIPLESHIP RESEARCH

Participants' Profiles Results

Item 1 of the Participant Profile asked for the participants' ages by age groups. The age categories were: 20–25 years, 26–35 years, 36–45 years, 46–55 years, and 65 years and above. There were 101 responses to this question. Table 1 displays the number of participants within the different age groups, as well as the percentages.

The largest age group consisted of individuals aged 46–55 years, with a total of 37 participants (36%). This result implies that young people exhibit a preference for small groups. The next largest age group consisted of individuals aged 20–25 years, with 24 participants (24%). This implies that young adults also have a preference for small groups. Next, the group of individuals aged 65 years and above showed 17 participants (17%). Then the age group of 36–45 years had 12 participants (12%). Finally, the age group of 26–35 years was shown to have 11 participants (11%).

Interpretations of the data presented in Table 1 are multifaceted. One possible explanation is that there is an increasing trend of older persons favoring small group settings. This phenomenon may be attributed to several sources. An alternative hypothesis is that there is a decline in the appeal of small groups among the younger adult demographic. There are several potential reasons for this phenomenon, including the growing prominence of other extracurricular options and missionary opportunities, as well as a perceived lack of relevance of the small group discipleship model among younger adults.

The data presented in Table 1 can also serve as a valuable resource for determining the age demographics of participants in small group settings. To illustrate: in the event that the platform aims to appeal to a larger demographic of younger adults, it might strategically prioritize incorporating elements that are highly sought-after by this specific age group, such as diverse categories of interests or hobbies. In general, the data presented in Table 1 offers significant insights on the age demographic of individuals involved in small group settings. These insights can be utilized to enhance the small group model and increase its attractiveness to a broader spectrum of consumers.

Table 1. Ages

Age Ranges	# of Responses	% of Responses
20–25 years old	24	24%
26–35 years old	11	11%
36–45 years old	12	12%
46–55 years old	37	36%
65 and above years	17	17%
Total	101	100%

Item 2 of the Participant Profile asked for the participants' genders. Table 2 below illustrates the distribution of the 100 survey replies. One column presents the number of responses for a gender category. The next column displays the percentage responses for a given gender category.

As shown in Table 2, Item 2 received a cumulative count of 100 replies. Out of that total sample, 32 respondents (32%) identified as male, 68 respondents (68%) identified as female, and no answers (0%) were received from persons who identified as intersex. The data presented in this table reveal that almost twice as many respondents identified as females compared with those who identified as males. The data presented in this table can also serve as valuable input for informing the design and implementation of the survey. For instance, in order to obtain a more precise depiction of a population, the survey could be given to a more equal number of females and males.

Table 2. Genders

Sex	# of Responses	% of Reponses
Male	32	32%
Female	68	68%
Intersex	0	0%
Total	100	100%

Item 3 of the Participant Profile asked for the participants' ethnicities, in order to ascertain their ethnic backgrounds. Table 3 below illustrates the number and percentage of replies from 101 participants. The findings indicated that 98 the respondents (97%) were Black. One respondent (1%) selected American Indian/Alaska Native, and 2 respondents (2%) selected Mixed Ethnicity. No respondents (0%) chose White, Asian, or Hawaiian/Pacific Islander.

The interpretations of the data presented in Table 3 are multifaceted. One potential hypothesis is that those who identify as Black may exhibit a higher propensity for engaging with small groups compared to those who identify as other ethnicities. This phenomenon may be attributed to various variables, including the demographic characteristic of black individuals being more inclined towards younger age groups and possessing greater accessibility. An alternative hypothesis posits that individuals of African descent exhibit a higher propensity to engage with small groups that prioritize matters pertaining to them.

The data presented in Table 3 can also serve as valuable insights for guiding the advancement of small groups. To illustrate: if the platform aims to enhance its appeal to those of non-Black descent, it could prioritize incorporating functionalities that resonate with the non-Black demographic. In general, the data presented here offers significant insights into the demographic characteristics of those utilizing small groups. These insights possess the potential to enhance the structure of the groups and increase its attractiveness to a broader spectrum of users.

Table 3. Ethnicities

Ethnicity	# of Responses	% of Responses
White	0	0%
Black	98	97%
Asian	0	0%
American Indian/Alaska Native	1	1%
Hawaiian/Pacific Islander	0	0%
Mixed Ethnicity	2	2%
Total	101	100%

Item 4 of the Participant Profile asked for the participants' employment status. According to Table 4, the largest portion of 78 respondents (78%) were engaged in full- time employment. This was followed by 10 respondents (10%) who were in part-time employment, and 12 respondents (12%) who were unemployed. This implied that the general employment condition within the research population was favorable.

There exist several potential rationales for the elevated quantity of individuals engaged in full-time employment. Initially, the research cohort may exhibit a concentration within sectors known for providing predominantly full-time employment opportunities (e.g. manufacturing or healthcare). Furthermore, it is worth noting that the study population may have possessed a high level of ability or expertise that rendered them particularly appealing to potential employers. Furthermore, the study population may have resided in a region that was characterized by a robust economic climate, which led to an increased availability of employment prospects.

The study findings indicated that a majority of individuals within the sample population were successful in securing full-time employment, as seen by the comparatively lower number of part-time respondents. Nevertheless, it is conceivable that certain individuals opt for part-time employment due to personal or financial motivations.

The limited quantity of individuals who were unemployed indicated a somewhat diminished level of unemployment within the examined community. This phenomenon may have been indicative of a favorable economic outlook, as it signified a higher rate of employment among individuals with the capacity to participate in the workforce. It may also include respondents who were retired or who did not need to be employed.

Table 4. Employment

Employment	# of Responses	% of Responses
Full-Time	78	78%
Part-Time	10	10%
Unemployed	12	12%
Total	100	100%

Item 5 of the Participant Profile asked for the participants' marital status. Table 5 indicates that the largest portion of respondents (51) categorized themselves as single, accounting for 51% of the respondents. This was followed by 40 individuals who were married, constituting 40% of the sample. A smaller number of respondents (6) reported being divorced (6%), while the remaining 3 respondents (3%) identified as widowed.

These results indicated that the majority of these small group respondents exhibited a notable prevalence of individuals who were not in a marital relationship.

Several potential explanations exist for these statistics. Notably, an increasing number of individuals are opting for cohabitation as opposed to entering matrimony. Additionally, there has been an increase in the number of individuals experiencing divorce. A prevalence of singlehood may carry several ramifications. For instance, this phenomenon may signify an increase in the number of individuals residing in solitary households, hence yielding a range of potential life outcomes that may be positive or negative. Additionally, this phenomenon may imply an increase in the number of individuals who are assuming the responsibility of child-rearing in the absence of a marital or even cohabitating partner, possibly presenting difficulties.

Table 5. Marital Status

Marital Status	# of Responses	% of Responses
Single	51	51%
Married	40	40%
Divorced	6	6%
Widowed	3	3%
Total	100	100%

Item 6 of the Participant Profile asked for the participants' education levels. There were 100 responses to this item. As shown in Table 6, the prevailing educational attainment was a high school diploma, which was reported by 48 respondents (48%). The rest of the responses indicated educational attainments as follows: GED by 6 respondents (6%), Associates Degree by 22 respondents (22%), Bachelors Degree by 14 respondents (14%), and Masters Degree by 10 respondents (10%). No respondents (0%) indicated Doctorate Degree.

These findings indicated that a significant proportion of the participants possessed a level of education of a high school diploma or a GED. This phenomenon may be attributed to the fact that many participants exhibited a commendable high school graduation rate. Nevertheless, it is important to acknowledge that there has also been a notable rise in the proportion of individuals attaining a higher education degree within the United States.

Several potential reasons can account for the educational achievements of the participants. Initially, it is plausible that the survey was administered among a demographic area that was characterized by a lower level of educational attainment, compared to the broader population. Furthermore, it is possible that the study was carried out in a geographical area that was characterized by relatively lower levels of educational achievement. Furthermore, it is plausible that the survey was administered exclusively to a particular demographic, such as individuals in the young adult age range or those with lower income levels, who may have exhibited a lower likelihood of possessing a collegiate education. The educational achievements of the participants may have many consequences. For instance, it may have an impact on their prospects for employment, their income levels, and their overall well-being. Furthermore, it has the potential to influence individuals' political ideologies and their engagement in civic endeavors.

Table 6. Education

Education Level	# of Responses	% of Responses
HS Diploma	48	48%
GED	6	6%
Associates Degree (A.A., A.S., etc.)	22	22%
Bachelors Degree (B.A., B.S., etc.)	14	14%
Masters Degree (M.A., M.S., etc.)	10	10%
Doctorate Degree (Ph.D., Ed.D., D. Min, Th.D.)	0	0%
Total	100	100%

Item 7 of the Participant Profile asked for: "Number of Small Groups attended that emphasized any topic of biblical teaching, education, life skills, or personal development." Table 7 illustrates the results. From the 99 responses, 26 respondents (26%) attended "One" of the described groups. Next, 15 respondents (15%) attended "Two" of the described groups. Then, 10 respondents (10%) attended "Three" of the described groups. The majority of 48 respondents (49%) attended "Four or More" of the described groups. These results imply that may be exist some level of interest among individuals to acquire further knowledge on the Bible. There also seems to be an inclination among individuals to acquire knowledge and skills that might effectively enhance their own well-being and daily functioning.

There exist several potential explanations for the various categories of small groups in which people partake. Initially, individuals may exhibit a heightened inclination towards acquiring knowledge pertaining to subjects that directly pertain to their personal experiences. Individuals with a keen interest in religion may exhibit a higher propensity to participate in a community that places significant emphasis on biblical instruction. Individuals with a vested interest in enhancing their professional trajectories may exhibit a higher propensity to engage in educational-oriented collectives. Individuals who possess a desire to enhance their personal lives may exhibit a higher propensity to participate in a group that places emphasis on the cultivation of life skills or personal development.

The presence of various categories of groups may also exert an influence. For instance, in the scenario where there exists a greater number of groups prioritizing biblical instruction compared to groups emphasizing education, it is likely that a larger proportion of individuals would choose to participate in the former. Additionally, the subjective inclinations of the individual may also exert influence. For instance, certain individuals may exhibit a preference for acquiring knowledge within a collective environment, whilst others may have a predilection for solo learning. Individuals may exhibit a preference for acquiring knowledge in areas that include practicality and direct applicability to their personal life, whereas others may have a preference for subjects that are more theoretical or abstract in nature.

Table 7. Number of Small Groups Attended that Emphasized Any Topic of Biblical Teaching, Education, Life Skills, or Personal Development

Number of Small Groups Attended	# of Responses	% of Responses
One	26	26%
Two	15	15%
Three	10	10%
Four or More	48	49%
Total	99	100%

SURVEY INSTRUMENT

1.   Rate how your cell group experience addresses the needs of the local church for the following: Accountability.
[ ] 1—Strongly Disagree [ ] 2—Disagree
[ ] 3—Neither Agree nor Disagree [ ] 4—Agree
[ ] 5—Strongly Agree

2.   Rate how your cell group experience addresses the needs of the local church for the following: Fellowship.
[ ] 1—Strongly Disagree [ ] 2—Disagree
[ ] 3—Neither Agree nor Disagree [ ] 4—Agree
[ ] 5—Strongly Agree

3.   Rate how your cell group experience addresses the needs of the local church for the following: Leadership Development.
[ ] 1—Strongly Disagree [ ] 2—Disagree
[ ] 3—Neither Agree nor Disagree [ ] 4—Agree
[ ] 5—Strongly Agree

4.   Rate how your cell group experience addresses the needs of the local church for the following: Charity/Service Work.
[ ] 1—Strongly Disagree [ ] 2—Disagree
[ ] 3—Neither Agree nor Disagree [ ] 4—Agree
[ ] 5—Strongly Agree

5.   Rate how your cell group experience addresses the needs of the local church for the following: Church Member Care and Engagement.
[ ] 1—Strongly Disagree [ ] 2—Disagree
[ ] 3—Neither Agree nor Disagree [ ] 4—Agree
[ ] 5—Strongly Agree

6. Rate how your cell group experience addresses the needs of the local church for the following: Organization by Leader.
[ ] 1—Strongly Disagree [ ] 2—Disagree
[ ] 3—Neither Agree nor Disagree [ ] 4—Agree
[ ] 5—Strongly Agree

7. Rate how your cell group experience addresses the needs of the local church for the following: Message Dissemination.
[ ] 1—Strongly Disagree [ ] 2—Disagree
[ ] 3—Neither Agree nor Disagree [ ] 4—Agree
[ ] 5—Strongly Agree

8. Rate how your cell group experience addresses the needs of the local church for the following: Impartation of Spiritual Gifts.
[ ] 1—Strongly Disagree [ ] 2—Disagree
[ ] 3—Neither Agree nor Disagree [ ] 4—Agree
[ ] 5—Strongly Agree

9. Rate how your cell group experience addresses the needs of the local church for the following: Increase of Church Attendance.
[ ] 1—Strongly Disagree [ ] 2—Disagree
[ ] 3—Neither Agree nor Disagree [ ] 4—Agree
[ ] 5—Strongly Agree

10. Rate how your cell group experience addresses the needs of the local church for the following: Intercessory Work.
[ ] 1—Strongly Disagree [ ] 2—Disagree
[ ] 3—Neither Agree nor Disagree [ ] 4—Agree
[ ] 5—Strongly Agree

11.   I am able to access Small Groups supplementary support resources at my church. [ ] 1—Strongly Disagree
[ ] 2—Disagree
[ ] 3—Neither Agree nor Disagree [ ] 4—Agree
[ ] 5—Strongly Agree

12.   Rate the increase of Tithes and Offerings since the implementation of small groups in your congregational setting.
[ ] 1—Not at all satisfied [ ] 2—Slightly Satisfied
[ ] 3—Moderately Satisfied [ ] 4—Very Satisfied
[ ] 5—Completely Satisfied

13.   Rate the increase in Church Attendance since the implementation of small groups in your congregational setting.
[ ] 1—Not at all satisfied [ ] 2—Slightly Satisfied
[ ] 3—Moderately Satisfied [ ] 4—Very Satisfied
[ ] 5—Completely Satisfied

14.   Rate the increase of the Volunteer Population since the implementation of small groups in your congregational setting.
[ ] 1—Not at all satisfied [ ] 2—Slightly Satisfied
[ ] 3—Moderately Satisfied [ ] 4—Very Satisfied
[ ] 5—Completely Satisfied

15.   Rate the increase in Fellowship Attendance (i.e.— Even during special events) since the implementation of small groups in your congregational setting.
[ ] 1—Not at all satisfied [ ] 2—Slightly Satisfied
[ ] 3—Moderately Satisfied [ ] 4—Very Satisfied
[ ] 5—Completely Satisfied

16. Rate the increase in Altar Calls since the implementation of small groups in your congregational setting.
[ ] 1—Not at all satisfied [ ] 2—Slightly Satisfied
[ ] 3—Moderately Satisfied [ ] 4—Very Satisfied
[ ] 5—Completely Satisfied

17. Rate the increase in Small Group Attendance since the implementation of small groups in your congregational setting.
[ ] 1—Not at all satisfied [ ] 2—Slightly Satisfied
[ ] 3—Moderately Satisfied [ ] 4—Very Satisfied
[ ] 5—Completely Satisfied

18. Rate the increase of Small Group Leaders since the implementation of small groups in your congregational setting.
[ ] 1—Not at all satisfied [ ] 2—Slightly Satisfied
[ ] 3—Moderately Satisfied [ ] 4—Very Satisfied
[ ] 5—Completely Satisfied

19. Rate the increase of Baptism Participants since the implementation of small groups in your congregational setting.
[ ] 1—Not at all satisfied [ ] 2—Slightly Satisfied
[ ] 3—Moderately Satisfied [ ] 4—Very Satisfied
[ ] 5—Completely Satisfied

Thanks for your commitment to ensuring that Lawrence L. Brandon provides insight to with the foundation of knowledge, skills, and character necessary to determine The Success of Small Groups as a Discipleship Model in the 21st Century Church.

Survey Instrument Results

Item 1 of the Survey Instrument was: "Rate how your cell group experience addresses the needs of the local church for the following: Accountability." As shown in Table 8 a significant portion of participants (43 or 42%) express agreement with this statement. The subsequent responses were as follows: 39 respondents (39%) strongly agreed, 7 respondents (7%) neither agreed nor disagreed, 2 respondents (2%) disagreed, and 10 respondents (10%) strongly disagreed.

This implied that a majority of those who engaged in cell groups held the belief that these organizations offered a significant avenue for fostering accountability. This aligns with the existing body of research. The research indicated that cell groups can serve as a viable method for offering support and motivation to participants, while also fostering a sense of responsibility towards their individual goals.

There are several potential rationales for the substantial

proportion of individuals who exhibited a strong concurrence with the efficacy of their cell group involvement in fulfilling the accountability requirements of the local church. Cell groups are commonly characterized by their small size and intimate nature, which facilitates the cultivation of trust and rapport among members. This has the potential to establish a secure and nurturing atmosphere in which individuals are at ease in divulging their difficulties and obstacles. Furthermore, cell groups generally convene on a regular basis, thereby affording members the opportunity to engage in regular check-ins with one another. This can facilitate the monitoring of members' adherence to their obligations and the identification of any challenges that they may encounter. Additionally, cell groups frequently exhibit a distinct emphasis on the cultivation and advancement of spiritual growth. This can serve as a catalyst for inspiring individuals to align their actions with their religious beliefs, while concurrently offering them the necessary assistance to surmount obstacles.

Table 8. Small Group Experience Addresses the Need for Accountability

Response Choices	# of Responses	% of Responses
Strongly Disagree	10	10%
Disagree	2	2%
Neither Agree nor Disagree	7	7%
Agree	43	42%
Strongly Agree	39	39%
Total	101	100%

Item 2 of the Survey Instrument was: "Rate how your cell group experience addresses the needs of the local church for the following: Fellowship." Table 9 illustrates the quantitative data pertaining to this. A significant proportion of participants (41 or 41%) expressed strong agreement, and 44 participants (43%) expressed agreement. The subsequent responses are categorized as follows: 5 respondents (5%) neither agreed nor disagreed, 2 respondents (2%) disagreed, and 9 respondents (9%) strongly disagreed.

This data indicates that a majority of individuals who engage in cell groups hold the belief that these organizations offer a significant avenue for fostering fellowship. This aligns with the existing body of research. The research posits that cell groups have the potential to serve as a viable mechanism for fostering interpersonal connections, offering assistance, and cultivating a communal atmosphere.

Several potential justifications exist for the substantial proportion of respondents who expressed a strong concurrence with the efficacy of their cell group involvement in addresses the fellowship needs of the local church. Initially, cell groups are commonly characterized by their modest size and intimate nature, facilitating the cultivation of strong interpersonal bonds among their participants. This can foster a secure and nurturing atmosphere in which individuals feel at ease expressing their authentic selves and engaging in open dialogue about their personal experiences with fellow members.

Additionally, cell groups commonly convene on a regular basis, facilitating regular gatherings for members to get together. This can help to strengthen relationships and create a sense of community. Additionally, cell groups frequently prioritize shared interests and activities, thus establishing a mutual foundation for members to establish connections with one another. This can facilitate the establishment of interpersonal connections and foster a feeling of inclusion.

Table 9. Small Group Experience Addresses the Need for Fellowship

Response Choices	# of Responses	% of Responses
Strongly Disagree	9	9%
Disagree	2	2%
Neither Agree nor Disagree	5	5%
Agree	44	43%
Strongly Agree	41	41%
Total	101	100%

Item 3 of the Survey Instrument was: "Rate how your cell group experience addresses the needs of the local church for the following: Leadership Development." Table 10 depicts the quantitative data regarding the responses for this. The results show that a significant proportion of participants expressed strong agreement (43 or 42.5%) and agreement (43 or 42.5%) regarding this statement. The rest of the responses were categorized as: 4 respondents (4%) neither agreed nor disagreed, 1 respondent (1%) disagreed, and 10 respondents (10%) strongly disagreed. These results imply that a majority of those who engaged in cell groups held the belief that such organizations offered potential for the development of leadership skills. Nevertheless, a notable proportion of individuals (15 or 15%) had divergent opinions, including a strong disagreement with Item 3.

There are several potential explanations for the substantial proportion of individuals who concurred that their cell group experience addresses the needs of the local church for leadership development. Cell groups are commonly characterized by their small size and close nature, hence affording members the chance to acquire and use leadership abilities. Furthermore, it is customary for cell groups to convene on a regular basis, thereby affording members the chance to receive constructive evaluations of their leadership aptitude from their peers. Additionally, it is common for cell groups to prioritize collective interests and engage in shared activities, thus creating an environment conducive to the cultivation of leadership abilities among its members. Nevertheless, there exist several potential justifications for the noteworthy subset of individuals who did not agree nor strongly agree with Item 3. It is possible that certain cell groups may not possess a deliberate design or facilitation that actively fosters the development of leadership skills. Moreover, certain cell groups may have a hierarchical structure whereby a small number of influential leaders hold significant power, thus hindering the growth of leadership abilities among other members. Additionally, certain cell groups may lack a distinct emphasis on the cultivation of spiritual growth and development, hence diminishing the likelihood of offering avenues for the nurturing of leadership skills.

Table 10. Small Group Experience Addresses the Need for Leadership Development

Response Choices	# of Responses	% of Responses
Strongly Disagree	10	10.0%
Disagree	1	1.0%
Neither Agree nor Disagree	4	4.0%
Agree	43	42.5%
Strongly Agree	43	42.5%
Total	101	100.0%

Item 4 of the Survey Instrument was: "Rate how your cell group experience addresses the needs of the local church for the following: Charity/Service Work." Table 11 displays the quantitative data pertaining to the responses. A significant proportion of participants expressed strong agreement (44 or 43%), and expressed agreement (41 or 41%). The rest of the responses were as follows: 4 respondents (4%) neither agreed nor disagreed, 2 respondents (2%) disagreed, and 10 respondents (10%) strongly disagreed.

This implies that a majority of those who engaged in cell groups held the belief that their cell group experience addresses the needs of the local church for charity/service work. These findings align with the existing body of research, which indicates that cell groups can serve as a viable means of facilitating individuals' engagement with community service activities.

There exist several potential rationales for the substantial proportion of individuals who expressed strong agreement and agreement with the efficacy of their cell group experience in addressing the charity/service work need of the local church.

Initially, cell groups are characterized by their modest size and close-knit nature, facilitating enhanced interpersonal connections among members, and enabling them to discern opportunities for engagement and contribution. Likewise, cell groups commonly convene on a regular basis, thus affording members the chance to engage in discussions and to strategize service initiatives. Furthermore, cell groups frequently prioritize common interests and activities, thereby establishing a conducive environment for members to engage in collaborative service. Nonetheless, there exist some potential justifications for the noteworthy subset of individuals who disagreed, strongly disagreed, or neither agreed nor disagreed with their cell group experience in addressing the charity/service work need of the local church.

Initially, it is important to acknowledge that certain cell groups may not include a deliberate structure or facilitation that actively encourages engagement in charitable or service-oriented endeavors. Likewise, certain cell groups may have a hierarchical structure characterized by a limited number of influential leaders, hence impeding the active participation of other members in service initiatives. Besides, certain cell groups may lack a distinct emphasis on addressing the requirements of the immediate community, hence diminishing the likelihood of their involvement in charitable or service-oriented endeavors.

Table 11. Small Group Experience Addresses the Need for Charity/Service Work

Response Choices	# of Responses	% of Responses
Strongly Disagree	10	10%
Disagree	2	2%
Neither Agree nor Disagree	4	4%
Agree	41	41%
Strongly Agree	44	43%
Total	101	100%

Item 5 of the Survey Instrument was: "Rate how your cell group experience addresses the needs of the local church for the following: Church Member Care and Engagement." Table 12 illustrates the data for the responses. As shown, 40 respondents (40.5%) strongly agreed, and 40 respondents (40.5%) agreed. The other responses consisted of: 8 respondents (8%) neither agreed nor disagreed, 4 respondents (4%) disagreed, and 7 respondents (7%) strongly disagreed.

These findings indicate that a majority of participants who engaged in cell groups held the belief that their cell group experience addresses the needs of the local church for church member care and engagement. This aligns with the existing body of research, which indicates that cell groups can serve as a viable method for fostering interpersonal connections among individuals, as well as for facilitating their engagement with the local religious community.

Several potential reasons exist for the substantial proportion of individuals who expressed agreement and strong agreement that their cell group experience addresses the needs of the local church in terms of member care and engagement. Cell groups are commonly characterized by their tiny size and intimate nature, facilitating a conducive environment for members to establish personal connections and foster relationships.

Additionally, cell groups commonly convene on a regular basis, thereby affording members the chance to engage in mutual communication and extend assistance to one another. Furthermore, cell groups frequently prioritize common interests and activities, thus establishing a framework for members to foster connections among themselves and with the local church.

Nevertheless, there exist several potential justifications for the notable subset of individuals who disagreed, strongly disagreed, or neither agreed nor disagreed with their cell group experience in addressing the church member care and engagement needs of the local church. Initially, it is worth noting that certain cell groups may lack purposeful design or facilitation that is aimed at fostering caring and involvement among church members. Furthermore, certain cell groups may have a hierarchical structure that is characterized by a limited number of influential leaders, hence impeding the participation of other members in caregiving and engagement endeavors. Additionally, certain cell groups may lack a distinct emphasis on addressing the specific requirements of the local church, thereby diminishing their likelihood of actively participating in the care and engagement of church members.

Table 12. Small Group Experience Addresses the Need for Church Member Care and Engagement

Response Choices	# of Responses	% of Responses
Strongly Disagree	7	7.0%
Disagree	4	4.0%
Neither Agree nor Disagree	8	8.0%
Agree	40	40.5%
Strongly Agree	40	40.5%
Total	99	100.0%

Item 6 of the Survey Instrument was: "Rate how your cell group experience addresses the needs of the local church for the following: Organization by Leader." Table 13 gives the results for this item. The data indicate that among the respondents, 8 individuals (8%) expressed strong disagreement, 3 individuals (3%) expressed disagree, 4 individuals (4%) either agreed nor disagreed, 36 individuals (36.5%) expressed agreement, and 48 individuals (48.5%) expressed strong agreement.

These findings imply that there was a diverse array of perspectives regarding the participants' cell group experience addressing the needs of the local church for organization by leader. A substantial proportion of participants (84 or 85%) expressed strong agreement or agreement with this idea. However, a notable minority (15 or 15%) held strong disagreement, disagreement, or neither agreed nor disagreed. There exist several potential rationales for the divergent perspectives around this matter. There is a perspective that advocates for a greater degree of structure and organization among cell groups, wherein a designated leader assumes the responsibility of orchestrating and guiding the groups' activities. Furthermore, it is arguable that certain individuals may advocate for a more casual and adaptable approach to cell groups, characterized by a reduced emphasis on hierarchical arrangements. It is also arguable that the efficacy of cell groups is not contingent upon the hierarchical structuring by a leader, but rather on the interpersonal connections and dynamics among the group members.

Table 13. Small Group Experience Addresses the Need for Organization by Leader

Response Choices	# of Responses	% of Responses
Strongly Disagree	8	8.0%
Disagree	3	3.0%
Neither Agree nor Disagree	4	4.0%
Agree	36	36.5%
Strongly Agree	48	48.5%
Total	99	100.0%

Item 7 of the Survey Instrument was: "Rate how your cell group experience addresses the needs of the local church for the following: Message Dissemination." Table 14 presents the data pertaining to the replies. The data indicate that 9 participants (9%) expressed strong disagreement, 4 participants (4%) expressed disagreement, 8 participants (8%) neither agreed nor disagreed, 38 participants (38.5%) expressed agreement, and 40 participants (40.5%) strongly agreed.

These results indicate that there existed a diverse array of perspectives regarding how participants' cell group experience addresses the needs of the local church for message dissemination. A substantial proportion of participants (78 or 79%) expressed strong agreement or agreement with this. However, although a notable minority (13 or 13%) held a contrary perspective.

Several potential rationales exist for the divergent perspectives around this matter.

Initially, it is arguable that cell groups serve as a viable method for effectively transmitting teachings from the local church to its members. Furthermore, there is a perspective that cell groups may not be a proficient means of transmitting information due to their typically limited size and informal nature. Additionally, it is possible that certain individuals hold the belief that the efficacy of message dissemination does not rely on cell groups, but rather on alternative elements, such as the caliber of the message and the manner in which it is sent.

Table 14. Small Group Experience Addresses the Need for Message Dissemination

Response Choices	# of Responses	% of Responses
Strongly Disagree	9	9.0%
Disagree	4	4.0%
Neither Agree nor Disagree	8	8.0%
Agree	38	38.5%
Strongly Agree	40	40.5%
Total	99	100.0%

Item 8 of the Survey Instrument was: "Rate how your cell group experience addresses the needs of the local church for the following: Impartation of Spiritual Gifts." Table 15 presents the results for this item. As shown, 46 respondents (46%) strongly agreed, 35 respondents (35%) agreed, 8 respondents (8%) neither agreed nor disagreed, 5 respondents (5%) disagreed, and 6 respondents (6%) disagreed.

These findings suggest that the majority of respondents (81%) strongly agree or agree that their cell group experience addresses the needs of the local church for the impartation of spiritual gifts. There are a few possible explanations for the high number of people who agree or strongly agree that their cell group experience addresses the needs of the local church for the impartation of spiritual gifts. First, cell groups are typically small and intimate groups, which can make it easier for members to share their spiritual gifts with each other. Second, cell groups typically meet regularly, which provides an opportunity for members to practice their spiritual gifts.

Third, cell groups often focus on shared interests and activities, which can provide a context for members to use their spiritual gifts.

However, 11% of respondents disagreed or strongly disagreed, and 8% neither agreed nor disagreed that their experience addresses the needs for impartation of spiritual gifts. There are some possible explanations for this noteworthy minority. First, some cell groups may not be designed or facilitated in a way that intentionally promotes the impartation of spiritual gifts. Second, some cell groups may be dominated by a few strong leaders, which may make it difficult for other members to develop and use their spiritual gifts. Third, some cell groups may not have a clear focus on spiritual growth and development, which may make it less likely that they will provide opportunities for the impartation of spiritual gifts.

Table 15. Small Group Experience Addresses the Need for Impartation of Spiritual Gifts

Response Choices	# of Responses	% of Responses
Strongly Disagree	6	6%
Disagree	5	5%
Neither Agree nor Disagree	8	8%
Agree	35	35%
Strongly Agree	46	46%
Total	100	100%

Item 9 of the Survey Instrument was: "Rate how your cell group experience addresses the needs of the local church for the following: Increase of Church Attendance." Table 16 displays the quantitative data for the responses. It reveals that 10 respondents (10%) strongly disagreed, 2 respondents (2%) disagreed, 8 respondents (8%) neither agreed nor disagreed, 45 respondents (45%) agreed, and 35 respondents (35%) strongly agreed.

The data indicate that a significant proportion of participants (80 or 85%) expressed strong agreement or agreement that their cell group experience addresses the needs of the local church for increasing church attendance. Several potential explanations exist for the substantial proportion of individuals who expressed strong agreement and agreement regarding their cell group experience addressing the needs of the local church for increasing church attendance. Cell groups are commonly characterized by their small size and intimate nature, facilitating a heightened sense of connection among members to the church. Additionally, cell groups often convene on a regular basis, thereby fostering the development of consistent church attendance patterns. Moreover, cell groups frequently prioritize common interests and activities, thus enhancing the overall experience of attending church.

Noteworthy is that 12 participants (12%) strongly disagreed or disagreed. Also noteworthy is that 8 participants (8%) neither agreed nor disagreed. There are several potential justifications for these stances toward the participants' cell group experience addressing the needs for increasing church attendance. It is plausible that certain cell groups may not be structured or guided with the explicit purpose of fostering church attendance. Additionally, certain cell groups may have a hierarchical structure characterized by a limited number of influential leaders, hence impeding the sense of inclusivity and belonging among other group members. Furthermore, certain cell groups may lack a distinct emphasis on the advancement of spiritual growth and development, hence diminishing the likelihood of facilitating possibilities for church attendance.

Table 16. Small Group Experience Addresses the Need for Increase of Church Attendance

Response Choices	# of Responses	% of Responses
Strongly Disagree	10	10%
Disagree	2	2%
Neither Agree nor Disagree	8	8%
Agree	45	45%
Strongly Agree	35	35%
Total	100	100%

Item 10 of the Survey Instrument was: "Rate how your cell group experience addresses the needs of the local church for the following: Intercessory Work." Table 17 gives the responses. The data indicate that among the respondents, 11 individuals (11%) expressed strong disagreement, 1 individual (1%) expressed disagreement, 9 individuals (9%) neither agreed nor disagreed, 38 individuals (37%) expressed agreement, and 43 individuals (42%) strongly agreed.

The data indicates that a significant proportion of participants (81 or 79%) expressed strong agreement or agreement that their cell group experience addresses the needs of the local church for intercessory work. There are several potential rationales for these positive responses. Cell groups are commonly characterized by their small and intimate nature, facilitating a conducive environment for members to express their prayer requests and concerns openly. Furthermore, it is customary for cell groups to convene on a regular basis, thereby affording members the chance to engage in intercessory prayer for one another, and for the various needs of the church community. What is more, cell groups frequently prioritize collective interests and engagements, thereby establishing a conducive environment for members to engage in communal prayer.

However, 21 respondents (21%) disagreed, strongly disagreed, or neither agreed nor disagreed that their cell group experience addresses the needs of the local church for intercessory work. There are several potential justifications for this noteworthy subset of individuals. Certain cell groups may lack purposeful design or facilitation to foster intercessory prayer. Additionally, certain cell groups may have a hierarchical structure wherein a small number of influential leaders exert significant control. This dynamic might potentially create an environment where other members may experience hesitancy in expressing their personal prayer needs. Furthermore, certain cell groups may lack a distinct emphasis on the cultivation of spiritual growth and development, hence reducing the likelihood of offering occasions for intercessory prayer.

Table 17. Small Group Experience Addresses the Need for Intercessory Work

Response Choices	# of Responses	% of Responses
Strongly Disagree	11	11%
Disagree	1	1%
Neither Agree nor Disagree	9	9%
Agree	38	37%
Strongly Agree	43	42%
Total	102	100%

Item 11 of the Survey Instrument was: "I am able to access Small Groups supplementary support resources at my church." Table 18 displays the quantitative data for the responses. The data indicate that out of the total respondents, 11 individuals (11%) strongly disagreed, 6 individuals (6%) disagreed, 12 individuals (12%) neither agreed nor disagreed, 35 individuals (34%) agreed, and 38 individuals (37%) strongly agreed. The results indicate that a significant proportion of participants (73 or 71%) expressed a strong agreement or agreement that they were able to access small groups supplementary support resources at their churches. Several potential reasons can account for this significant proportion. Cell groups are commonly characterized by their small size and intimate nature, facilitating a conducive environment for members to openly express their own wants and problems. Furthermore, cell groups commonly convene on a regular basis, so affording members the chance to acquire knowledge and avail themselves of additional support services. Additionally, cell groups frequently prioritize common interests and engagements, hence establishing a conducive environment for members to offer mutual assistance.

Noteworthy, though, was that 29 participants (29%) strongly disagreed, disagreed, or neither agreed nor disagreed that they were able to access small groups supplementary support resources at their churches. Several potential justifications are presented for these responses. It is possible that certain cell groups may lack purposeful design or facilitation aimed at promoting access to supplemental support services. Also, certain cell groups may have a hierarchical structure wherein a small number of influential leaders hold significant power, thereby impeding the ability of other members to express their demands and concerns openly. Furthermore, certain cell groups may lack a distinct emphasis on the enhancement of spiritual growth and development, hence reducing the likelihood of offering avenues for accessing further supportive resources.

Table 18. Able to Access Small Groups Supplementary Resources at My Church

Response Choices	# of Responses	% of Responses
Strongly Disagree	11	11%
Disagree	6	6%
Neither Agree nor Disagree	12	12%
Agree	35	34%
Strongly Agree	38	37%
Total	102	100%

Item 12 of the Survey Instrument was: "Rate the increase of Tithes and Offerings since the implementation of small groups in your congregational setting." Table 19 presents the responses to this. The majority of the 102 respondents (33 or 32%) were "Completely Satisfied" with the increase, followed by 32 respondents (31%) who were "Very Satisfied." then 29 respondents (29%) were "Moderately Satisfied." Only 4 respondents (4%) each were "Slightly Satisfied" and "Not At All Satisfied."

These results indicate that the implementation of small groups generally had been successful in increasing tithes and offerings, and that the respondents generally had some level of satisfaction with the results. It is essential to note, however, that this is a small survey, and the results may not apply to all congregational settings. It is also essential to consider other factors that may have contributed to the increase in tithes and offerings, such as the overall economic climate of the church.

Table 19. Increase of Tithes and Offerings Since Implementing Small Groups

Response Choices	# of Responses	% of Responses
Not At All Satisfied	4	4%
Slightly Satisfied	4	4%
Moderately Satisfied	29	29%
Very Satisfied	32	31%
Completely Satisfied	33	32%
Total	102	100%

Item 13 of the Survey Instrument was: "Rate the increase in Church Attendance since the implementation of small groups in your congregational setting." Table 20 illustrates the pertinent quantitative data. The results reveal that 3 respondents (3%) marked "Not at all satisfied," 7 respondents (7%) marked "Slightly Satisfied," 26 respondents (26%) marked "Moderately Satisfied," 29 respondents (29%) marked "Very Satisfied," and 36 respondents (35%) marked "Completely Satisfied."

These findings indicates that a significant proportion of participants (65 or 64%) expressed being completely satisfied or very satisfied with the increase in church attendance since the implementation of small groups in their congregational settings.

Several potential justifications exist for these notable degrees of contentment. Initially, the establishment of small groups can foster a more intimate and inclusive atmosphere, facilitating interpersonal connections among individuals and their affiliation with the religious community. Furthermore, small groups provide individuals with the chance to engage in activities and ministries aligned with their personal interests. Moreover, the establishment of small groups fosters a feeling of community and provides individuals with necessary support, hence promoting increased church attendance.

The rest of the responses showed that 36 respondents (36%) indicated moderate satisfaction, slight satisfaction, or no satisfaction at all concerning the increase in church attendance since the implementation of small groups in their congregational settings.

There are several potential justifications for participants expressing less or no satisfaction. Initially, it is worth noting that certain individuals may exhibit a lack of interest in engaging in small group activities. Furthermore, there may be individuals who perceive that small groups are not adequately addressing their requirements. Additionally, there may be a lack of awareness among certain individuals regarding the potential benefits and opportunities that can arise from engaging in small group settings.

Table 20. Increase in Church Attendance Since Implementing Small Groups

Response Choices	# of Responses	% of Responses
Not At All Satisfied	3	3%
Slightly Satisfied	7	7%
Moderately Satisfied	26	26%
Very Satisfied	29	29%
Completely Satisfied	36	35%
Total	101	100%

Item 14 of the Survey Instrument was: "Rate the increase of the Volunteer Population since the implementation of small groups in your congregational setting." Table 21 presents the quantity of responses. The data indicate that among the respondents, 5 individuals (5%) expressed "Not at all satisfied," 6 individuals (6%) marked "Slightly Satisfied," 22 individuals (22%) indicated "Moderately Satisfied," 41 individuals (40%) conveyed "Very Satisfied," and 28 individuals (27%) expressed "Completely Satisfied."

These finding indicate that a significant proportion of participants (69 or 67%) were completely satisfied or very satisfied with the increase of the volunteer population since implementing small groups in their congregational settings. Also indicated was that 33 participants (33%) expressed only moderate satisfaction, slight satisfaction, or no satisfaction at all. Several potential reasons can account for the notable degree of "Very Satisfied" and "Completely Satisfied" responses on the rise in the number of volunteers. The establishment of small groups can foster a setting that is characterized by intimacy and inclusivity, thereby facilitating interpersonal connections among individuals and their affiliation with the religious institution.

Table 21. Increase of Volunteer Population Since Implementing Small Groups

Response Choices	# of Responses	% of Responses
Not At All Satisfied	5	5%
Slightly Satisfied	6	6%
Moderately Satisfied	22	22%
Very Satisfied	41	40%
Completely Satisfied	28	27%
Total	102	100%

Item 15 of the Survey Instrument was: "Rate the increase in Fellowship Attendance (i.e.—Even during special events) since the implementation of small groups in your congregational setting." Table 22 illustrates the of replies received. The data indicate that 2 participants (2%) expressed "Not at all satisfied," 5 participants (5%) reported "Slightly Satisfied," 32 respondents (31%) indicated "Moderately Satisfied," 29 participants (29%) conveyed "Very Satisfied," and 34 individuals (33%) expressed "Completely Satisfied." These findings indicate that a significant proportion of participants (63 or 62%) expressed complete satisfaction or being very satisfied with the increase in fellowship attendance since implementing small groups in their congregational settings. Several potential justifications exist for this notable level of satisfaction. The formation of small groups can foster a sense of intimacy and inclusivity, enabling individuals to establish meaningful connections both among themselves and with the ecclesiastical community. Furthermore, the formation of small groups presents individuals with the chance to engage in activities and ministries aligned with their personal interests. Also, the establishment of small groups fosters a sense of community and offers individuals a support system, hence promoting increased participation in fellowship events. At the same time, 31% of respondents indicated only moderate satisfaction, 5% expressed only slight satisfaction, and 2% expressed being not at all satisfied with the increase in fellowship attendance since implementing small groups in their congregational settings. Potential justifications for these responses are as follows: It is plausible that certain individuals may lack enthusiasm or inclination towards participating in fellowship gatherings. Furthermore, there may be individuals who perceive that small groups are not adequately fulfilling their requirements. It is also worth noting that certain individuals may lack awareness regarding the potential for fellowship that small groups might provide.

Table 22. Increase in Fellowship Attendance Since Implementing Small Groups

Response Choices	# of Responses	% of Responses
Not At All Satisfied	2	2%
Slightly Satisfied	5	5%
Moderately Satisfied	32	31%
Very Satisfied	29	29%
Completely Satisfied	34	33%
Total	102	100%

Item 16 of the Survey Instrument was: "Rate the increase in Altar Calls since the implementation of small groups in your congregational setting." Table 23 provides the quantity of replies for this. The data indicate that 1 participant (1%) chose "Not at all satisfied," 4 participants (4%) expressed "Slightly Satisfied," 20 participants (20%) indicated "Moderately Satisfied," 40 participants (39%) marked "Very Satisfied," and 37 participants (36%) expressed "Completely Satisfied."

These findings indicate that a significant proportion of participants (77 or 75%) expressed being completely or very satisfied with the increase in altar calls since implementing small groups in their congregational settings. Several potential justifications exist for this notable degree of satisfaction. The formation of small groups can facilitate a setting that is characterized by a sense of intimacy and inclusivity, thereby enabling individuals to express their spiritual needs and concerns openly. Additionally, the formation of small groups provides individuals with the chance to engage in intercessory prayer, both for one another and for the various needs of the church community. Moreover, the establishment of small groups fosters a sense of community and offers individuals a support system, perhaps motivating them to react to altar calls. However, a noteworthy proportion of participants (25 or 25%) expressed only moderate satisfaction, slight satisfaction, or no satisfaction at all with the increase in altar calls since implementing small groups in their congregational settings. It is worth considering a few potential rationales for these participants' responses. It is plausible that certain individuals may exhibit a lack of interest in participating in altar calls.

Furthermore, it is plausible that certain individuals may have unease when it comes to disclosing their spiritual wants and worries within the context of a small-group environment. There also exists a lack of awareness among certain individuals regarding the potential benefits that small groups provide in terms of responding to altar calls.

Table 23. Increase in Altar Calls Since Implementing Small Groups

Response Choices	# of Responses	% of Responses
Not At All Satisfied	1	1%
Slightly Satisfied	4	4%
Moderately Satisfied	20	20%
Very Satisfied	40	39%
Completely Satisfied	37	36%
Total	102	100%

Item 17 of the Survey Instrument was: "Rate the increase in Small Group Attendance since the implementation of small groups in your congregational setting." Table 24 provides the statistics for this. The data show that 2 participants (2%) marked "Not at all satisfied," 7 participants (7%) reported "Slightly Satisfied," 23 participants (23%) indicated "Moderately Satisfied," 36 participants (35%) chose "Very Satisfied," and 33 participants (33%) selected "Completely Satisfied."

These findings indicate that a significant proportion of participants (69 or 68%) expressed being completely satisfied or very satisfied with the increase in small group attendance since implementing small groups in their congregational settings. Several potential reasons can account for these responses. The establishment of small groups can foster a more intimate and inclusive atmosphere, facilitating interpersonal connections among individuals and their affiliation with the religious institution. Furthermore, small groups provide individuals with the chance to engage in activities and ministries aligned with their personal interests. Additionally, the establishment of small groups fosters a sense of camaraderie and assistance among individuals, hence promoting increased participation in such groups. The findings also indicate that a noteworthy proportion of participants (32 or 32%) expressed being only moderately satisfied, slightly satisfied, or not at all satisfied with the increase in small group attendance since implementing small groups in their congregational settings. The responses of these participants may be attributed to the plausibility that certain individuals may exhibit a lack of interest in engaging in small group activities.

Table 24. Increase in Small Group Attendance Since Implementing Small Groups

Response Choices	# of Responses	% of Responses
Not At All Satisfied	2	2%
Slightly Satisfied	7	7%
Moderately Satisfied	23	23%
Very Satisfied	36	35%
Completely Satisfied	33	33%
Total	101	100%

Item 18 of the Survey Instrument was: "Rate the increase of Small Group Leaders since the implementation of small groups in your congregational setting." Table 25 illustrates the quantity and percentage of replies received in relation to this. Out of 101 respondents, 32 participants (32%) were "Completely Satisfied," 38 participants (37%) were "Very Satisfied," 20 participants (20%) were "Moderately Satisfied," 9 participants (9%) were "Slightly Satisfied," and 2 participants (2%) were "Not at all satisfied."

These results demonstrate that a significant majority of respondents expressed some level of satisfaction with the increase of small group leaders subsequent to introducing of small groups within the congregational context. In general, the findings of the survey indicate favorable outcomes for the church concerning the increase of small group leaders in their congregational setting.

Table 25. Increase of Small Group Leaders Since Implementing Small Groups

Response Choices	# of Responses	% of Responses
Not At All Satisfied	2	2%
Slightly Satisfied	9	9%
Moderately Satisfied	20	20%
Very Satisfied	38	37%
Completely Satisfied	32	32%
Total	101	100%

Item 19 of the Survey Instrument was: "Rate the increase of Baptism Participants since the implementation of small groups in your congregational setting." Table 26 shows the responses to this item. Out of 101 respondents, 3 respondents (3%) answered "Not at all satisfied," 11 participants (11%) answered "Slightly Satisfied," 21 participants (21%) answered "Moderately Satisfied," 35 participants (34%) answered "Very Satisfied," and 31 participants (31%) answered "Completely Satisfied." This illustrates that the majority of respondents (85 or 86%) were "completely," "very" or "moderately" satisfied with the increase in baptism participants. Another 21 participants (21%) at least were "slightly satisfied."

This implies that the incorporation of small groups yielded a favorable influence on the quantity of individuals participating in baptisms inside this religious community. Nonetheless, it is worth noting that there were 11 respondents who expressed being only "slightly satisfied" with the observed rise in baptism participants. Additionally, a smaller group of 3 respondents (3%) indicated no satisfaction all. This implies that there remains potential for enhancement, and it may be necessary for the congregation to persist in allocating resources towards small groups in order to observe further increases in baptisms.

Table 26. Increase of Baptism Participants Since Implementing Small Groups

Response Choices	# of Responses	% of Responses
Not At All Satisfied	3	3%
Slightly Satisfied	11	11%
Moderately Satisfied	21	21%
Very Satisfied	35	34%
Completely Satisfied	31	31%
Total	101	100%

Summary of Results

This project examined perspectives on small groups among 100 participants from a church congregation. The findings from the participants' profiles provided valuable insights into the demographic makeup of these small group participants and their views on the effectiveness of these groups. The participants' profiles revealed a significant proportion were aged 46–55, with young adults aged 20–25 also well represented. This points to an appeal across both older and younger demographics. Most respondents were female and identified as Black, implying potential avenues to expand appeal to males and non-Black individuals. Additionally, most participants were employed full-time and had a high school education, suggesting small groups engage those with modest academic credentials.

Regarding views on small groups, most respondents agreed that these settings provided fellowship, accountability, leadership development, charitable opportunities, and spiritual growth. Many also were satisfied with increased church engagement after introducing small groups. This aligns with research showing the effectiveness of these groups for fostering connections and community participation.

However, dissenting perspectives emerged. A subset of participants were concerned about the ability of small groups to address organizational needs, to disseminate information, and to facilitate access to church resources. This highlights areas where small groups may require reassessment and refinement.

Overall, the favorable opinions expressed by most participants underscored the valuable role that small groups can play within a modern ministry setting. As an intimate, interest-oriented gathering that convenes regularly, these groups possess clear potential to enrich disciples' development. Nevertheless, ensuring that groups address the full spectrum of congregants' requirements remains an essential consideration for successful integration.

In the survey instrument, this project examined perspectives of 100 participants on whether small groups effectively addressed various needs within their church community. The findings revealed predominantly favorable views concerning the ability of these groups to fulfill critical requirements. Regarding fellowship and accountability, over 80% of respondents agreed that small groups capably provided for these needs.

Strong majorities also endorsed the efficacy of these settings for enabling leadership development, charitable work, spiritual growth, and interpersonal care. Furthermore, most participants expressed satisfaction with subsequent increases in areas like church attendance, altar calls, and group participation.

However, dissenting perspectives emerged among a minority of participants on certain issues. Around 15% disagreed that groups address needs for leadership development and for access to church resources. Similar portions felt that groups failed to fulfill organizational, communication, and intercessory requirements.

The disagreements highlight areas requiring reassessment, like intentionally facilitating skill-building and prayer support. Nevertheless, the largely positive opinions underscore that intimate, interest-oriented small groups can enrich disciples' development. The key consideration remains ensuring that groups address the diversity of members' needs through inclusive programming.

Overall, small groups demonstrated significant promise for meeting multifaceted requirements within a modern ministry environment. However, actualizing their full potential necessitates continually evaluating their alignment with the evolving priorities of all congregants based on transparent feedback.

Project Conclusion

The project aimed to examine the effectiveness of small groups as a discipleship model in contemporary church settings. To achieve this, the perspectives of 100 members of such groups were surveyed with regard to their capacity to attend to vital spiritual and communal requirements. The results of the study indicated that substantial majorities held the belief that small groups effectively served crucial purposes, such as promoting camaraderie and responsibility, facilitating the growth of leaders and philanthropy, encouraging spiritual advancement, and strengthening interpersonal connections. These favorable evaluations are consistent with prior research that emphasized the potential of small, interest-driven groups to foster the growth of disciples through interdependent connections.

Nevertheless, opposing perspectives surfaced among a subset of participants.

Minorities of participants, comprising a range of about 10% to

15%, specifically indicated that small groups failed to fulfill the organizational, communication, resource access, and intercessory needs of the church. This feedback underscores certain aspects that necessitate continuous improvement, including the need for organizational supervision, effective information dissemination, financial support, and a greater emphasis on prayer. However, the overall sentiments suggest that participants hold a tremendous belief in the potential of small groups to foster comprehensive member care when implemented with careful consideration.

In summary, the results affirm the effectiveness of small groups as a discipleship strategy in the moving ministry landscape of the 21st century. The efficacy of these environments in promoting transformative spiritual development, which is forged through accountability and fellowship, was broadly endorsed by the participants. Church leaders are obligated to further enhance supportive organizational structures in order to maintain the vitality of groups. Moreover, in order to improve the responsiveness of groups to emerging requirements, it is critical to utilize the constructive criticisms of participants by engaging in ongoing evaluation and learning. The deliberate enhancement of identified shortcomings has the potential to magnify the already significant contributions that organizations make to the enrichment of their members. In summary, churches that have a flourishing ecosystem of small groups that prioritize spiritual growth and care are strategically positioned to cultivate disciples who are actively involved and energized in the twenty-first century.

Although most research supports the efficacy of small groups, success does not necessarily indicate a consistent and extensive transformative effect. Proficient pastors recognize the existence of a continuum extending from mere ceremonial engagement to a genuine transformation of one's spiritual existence. Metrics based on attendance and self- reported satisfaction are inadequate measures to assess the groups' ability to inspire profound personal transformations. Nonetheless, by attentively facilitating members' subtle signals with sensitivity, the atmosphere maintains the capacity for significant breakthroughs. One could say that beautiful things emerge when the Spirit moves through our sincerity, brokenness, and compassion for one another.

Systems for Leadership Development

The cultivation of well-prepared and receptive ministry leaders constitutes a critical element in the success of organizations. Implementing specialized leadership pipelines enables point individuals to receive ongoing coaching, problem-solving, and vision-setting. Instead of pursuing isolated objectives, groups flourish by means of networking. The researcher cannot overstate the significance of equipping leaders on the ground to champion the purposes of their groups. Ongoing summits that nourish leadership abilities and address common obstacles are invaluable for sustaining groups during the unavoidable transitions of the church.

Integrated Ecosystems for Discipleship

Isolated programs offer only partial resolutions, whereas interconnected systems revolutionize issues for good. By situating groups as cohesive elements within comprehensive discipleship pathways, their influence is significantly enhanced. In conjunction with mentorships, devotional gatherings, and mission opportunities, groups foster multidimensional maturation through the establishment of ecosystems guided by unified visions. This integration attains the continuity and profundity that are essential for fostering disciples for life. Disciples who are equipped to serve, lead, and represent the faith constitute the fruit.

In summary, ongoing support for the effective execution of the small group model is warranted via investments in leadership development pipelines, facilitator skills enhancement, and integration into comprehensive discipleship ecosystems. When maintained with diligence and foresight, their potential to significantly revolutionize contemporary religious communities is limitless.

Propagating Fertile Discipleship Ecosystems

Pastors and ministry leaders foster the conditions for organic flourishing by cultivating, rather than by exerting control over prospering small group models.

Transitioning from prescription to facilitation is crucial for advancement. Getting out of the way is the most difficult and crucial step. This involves resisting the urge to micromanage, as well as concentrating on encouraging self-organization. Critical components encompass establishing a theological foundation, nurturing relational soil via modeling, and offering a shield during periods of susceptibility.

Leaders are cultivators, not enforcers of results; they prepare the soil, plant seeds of vision, and supply the necessary nutrients for those seeds to germinate at the appropriate juncture. A useful methodology would be to cultivate an atmosphere of grace in order to foster genuine community. It is imperative to adjust conditions in these tiny ecosystems so that disciples may flourish. Leaders may supplement natural processes by tactfully incorporating guidance on speaking truth and spiritual risk-taking, while also exercising discernment regarding when to retreat. The resultant effect is the emergence of small, spiritually supportive gatherings that take ownership of their shared mission.

In summary, an interventionist stance inhibits the natural development of significant small groups. However, when servant leaders serve as enabling catalysts, then the dynamic potential of the model is unlocked. Through the acts of meekly preparing fertile ground, furnishing protection, and offering gentle course corrections, servant leaders establish the fundamental components that foster the growth and success of genuine discipleship communities. Within such contexts, the biblical ideal of koinonia fellowship is actualized as adherents shoulder one another's burdens in an effort to attain Christlikeness. The 21st century church is in dire need of such spiritual formation incubators.

BIBLIOGRAPHY

Books

Anderson, Keith R., and Randy D. Reese. *Spiritual Mentoring: A Guide for Seeking and Giving Direction.* Downers Grove, IL: InterVarsity Press, 1999.

Barlow, T. Ed. *Small Group Ministry in the Contemporary Church.* Independence, MO: Herald Publishing, 1972.

Borthwick, Paul. *New Directions for Small-Group Ministry.* Loveland, CO: Vital Ministry, 1999.

Bray, Gerald. *Biblical Interpretation: Past and Present.* Downers Grove, IL: InterVarsity Press, 1996.

Carter, Robert T., Tamara R. Buckley, and Schekeva P. Hall. "Racial Harassment in American Schools." In *Handbook of School Counseling*, ed. Hardin L. K. Coleman and Christine Yeh, 111-126. New York: Routledge, 2011.

Casteel, John L. *Spiritual Renewal Through Personal Groups.* New York: Association Press, 1957.

Cerna, Miguel Angel. *The Power of Small Groups in the Church.* Newbury Park, CA: El Camino, 1991.

Cohen, David. "Behaviorism." *The Oxford Companion to the Mind.* Edited by Richard L. Gregory. New York: Oxford University Press, 1987. 71.

Donahue, Bill, and Russ Robinson. *Building a Church of Small Groups: A Place Where Nobody Stands Alone.* Grand Rapids: Zondervan, 2001.
Dudley, Carl S. *Effective the Small Churches in the*

Twenty-First Century. Nashville: Abingdon Press, 2003.

Epp, Albert H. *Discipleship Therapy: Healthy Christians, Healthy Churches*. Henderson, NE: Stairway Discipleship, 1993.

Evans, Robert. *The Human Side of School Change: Reform, Resistance, and the Real-Life Problems of Innovation*. San Francisco: Jossey-Bass, 1996.

Frazee, Randy. *The Connecting Church: Beyond Small Groups to Authentic Community*. Grand Rapids: Zondervan, 2001.

Galloway, Dale E. *The Small Group Book: The Practical Guide for Nurturing Christians and Building Churches*, with Kathi Mills. Grand Rapids: Fleming H. Revell, 1995.

George, Carl F. *Prepare Your Church for the Future*. Grand Rapids, MI: Fleming H. Revell, 1992.

Glatz, Greg G. "2. Getting Past Stalled and Dissatisfied." In *The Great Co-Mission*. N.p.: n.p., 2014. https://greatcomission.pressbooks.com/chapter/getting-past-stalled-and-dissatisfied/ (5 February 2021).

Graham, George. "Behaviorism." *The Stanford Encyclopedia of Philosophy*. Spring 2019 ed. Edited by Edward N. Zalta. https://plato.stanford.edu/archives/spr2019/entries/behaviorism/ (5 February 2021).

Hillner, Kenneth P. *History and Systems of Modern Psychology: A Conceptual Approach*. New York: Gardner Press, 1984.

Hull, Bill. *The Disciple-Making Church: Leading a Body of Believers on the Journey of Faith*. Grand Rapids, MI: Fleming H. Revell, 1990.

Hunter, George G., III. *Church for the Unchurched: The Rebirth of "Apostolic Congregations" across the American Mission Field*. Nashville: Abingdon Press, 1996.

Hybels, Lynne, and Bill Hybels. *Rediscovering Church: The Story and Vision of Willow Creek Community Church*. Grand Rapids: Zondervan, 1995.

Icenogle, Gareth Weldon. *Biblical Foundations for Small Group Ministry: An Integrational Approach*. Downers Grove, IL: InterVarsity Press, 1994.

Jones, John E. "Types of Growth Groups." In *The Pfeiffer Library*. Vol. 13. 2nd ed. San Francisco: Jossey-Bass/Pfeiffer, 1998. 1-9.

Jones, Stanley E., Dean C. Barnlund, and Franklyn S. Haiman. *The Dynamics of Discussion: Communication in Small Groups*. 2nd ed. New York: HarperCollins, 1980.

Kirkpatrick, Thomas G. *Small Groups in the Church: A Handbook for Creating Community*. New York: Alban Institute, 1995.

Kuh, George D., and Ken O'Donnell. *Ensuring Quality and Taking High-Impact Practices to Scale*. Washington, DC: AAC&U, 2013.

Lavin, Ronald J. *Way to Grow: Dynamic Church Growth through Small Groups*. Lima, OH: CSS Publishing, 1996.

Levesque, Raynald, and SPSS Inc. *SPSS Programming and*

Data Management: A Guide for SPSS and SAS Users. 4th ed. Chicago: SPSS, Inc., 2007.

Lewis, Pamela S., Stephen H. Goodman, Patricia M. Fandt, and Joseph F. Michlitsch. *Management: Challenges for Tomorrow's Leaders*. 4th ed. Mason, OH: Thomson Learning, 2004.

Mahaney, C. J. "Why Small Groups?" In *Why Small Groups?* ed. C. J. Mahaney, 1-16. Gaithersburg, MD: Sovereign Grace Ministries, 1996.

Mallison, John. *Building Small Groups in the Christian Community*. West Ryde, NSW: Renewal Publications, 1979.

Manskar, Steven W. *Small-Group Ministries: Christian Formation through Mutual Accountability*. Nashville: Cokesbury, 2012.

Martin, Glen, and Gary McIntosh. *Creating Community: Deeper Fellowship through Small Group Ministry*. Nashville: Broadman & Holman, 1997.

Maybin, Janet, Neil Mercer, and Barry Stierer. "'Scaffolding': Learning in the Classroom." In *Thinking Voices: The Work of the National Oracy Project*, ed. Kate Norman, 186-195. London: Hodder & Stoughton, 1992.

McGavran, Donald A., and Win Arn. *How to Grow a Church*. Grand Rapids: Gospel Light, 1973.

McIntosh, Gary L. *One Size Doesn't Fit All: Bringing out the Best in Any Size Church*. Grand Rapids: Fleming H. Revell, 1999.

Montoya, Alex D. "Approaching Pastoral Ministry Scripturally." In *Rediscovering Pastoral Ministry: Shaping Ministry with Biblical Mandates*, ed. John MacArthur Jr., 64-83. Dallas: Word Publishing, 1995.

Mooney, Carol Garhart. *Theories of Childhood: An Introduction to Dewey, Montessori, Erikson, Piaget & Vygotsky*. St. Paul, MN: Redleaf, 2000.

Navigators, The. *The State of Discipleship*. Ventura, CA: Barna Group, 2015.

Niemandt, Nelus. *Missional Leadership*. HTS Religion and Society Series. Vol. 7. Cape Town, SA: AOSIS, 2019.

Novak, Christopher. *Conquering Adversity: Six Strategies to Move You and Your Team through Tough Times*. Dallas: CornerStone Leadership Institute, 2004.

Pocock, Michael, and Joseph Henriques. *Cultural Change and Your Church: Helping Your Church Thrive in a Diverse Society*. Grand Rapids: Baker Books, 2002.

Ragins, Belle Rose, and Kathy E. Kram. "The Roots and Meaning of Mentoring." In *The Handbook of Mentoring at Work: Theory, Research and Practice*, eds. Belle Rose Ragins and Kathy E. Kram, 3-16. Los Angeles: Sage Publications, 2007.

Schaal, David, and Ron Harmon, eds. *Community of Christ: Pastors and Leaders Field Guide*. Independence, MO: Herald Publishing House, 2012. https://www.cofchrist.org/common/cms/resources/Documents/pastors-and-leaders-field- guide.pdf (5 February 2021).

Smith, Donald P. *Empowering Ministry: Ways to Grow in Effectiveness*. Louisville: Westminster John Knox, 1996.

Sofield, Loughlan, and Carroll Juliano. *Collaboration: Uniting Our Gifts in Ministry*. Notre Dame, IN: Ave Maria Press, 2000.

Somerville, Greg. "Take This Group and Own It!" In *Why Small Groups?* ed. C. J. Mahaney, 31-43. Gaithersburg, MD: Sovereign Grace Ministries, 1996.

Spitters, Denny, and Mathew Ellison. *When Everything is Missions*. Orlando, FL: BottomLine Media, 2017.

Terry, John Mark. *Evangelism: A Concise History*. Nashville: Broadman & Holman, 1998.

Warren, Rick. *40 Days of Community Study Guide*. Grand Rapids: Zondervan, 2012.

_____. *The Purpose-Driven Church*. Grand Rapids: Zondervan, 1995.

Whitney, William B., and Pamela Ebstyne King. "Religious Congregations and Communities." In *Emerging Adults' Religiousness and Spirituality: Meaning- Making in an Age of Transition*, ed. Carolyn McNamara Barry and Mona M. Abo- Zena, 133-151. New York: Oxford University Press, 2014.

Zuriff, Gerald E. *Behaviorism: A Conceptual Reconstruction*. New York: Columbia University Press, 1985.

Periodicals

Cushman, Jennifer E., Miriah Russo Kelly, Maryann Fusco-Rollins, and Ryan Faulkner. "Resource Review—Using Qualtrics Core XM for Surveying Youth." *Journal of Youth*

Development 16, no. 1 (2021): 161-167. https://jyd.pitt.edu/ojs/jyd/article/view/21-16-1-RR-3/1231 (28 August 2022).

Faraoanu, Iulian. "The Call and Mission of the Disciple in the Gospel According to Mark." *International Letters of Social and Humanistic Sciences* 60 (September 2015): 67-76. https://pdfs.semanticscholar.org/90e1/1c266b88bd4174e88485c0e571f73377c365.pdf?_ga=2.14100606.874651925.1613417265-309685894.1613417265 (5 February 2021).

Lamport, Mark A., and Mary Rynsburger. "All the Rage: How Small Groups are Really Educating Christian Adults; Part 2: Augmenting Small Group Ministry Practice—Developing Small Group Leadership Skills through Insights from Cognate Theoretical Disciplines." *Christian Education Journal* 5, no. 2 (2008): 391-414.

Makewa, Lazarus Ndiku, Dorcas Gitonga, Baraka Ngussa, Samwel Njoroge, and Joshua Kuboja. "Frustration Factor in Group Collaborative Learning Experiences." *American Journal of Educational Research* 2, no. 11A (2014): 16-22. https://www.researchgate.net/publication/269334783_Frustration_Factor_in_Group_ Collaborative_Learning_Experiences (5 February 2021).

McIntosh, Gary L. "Reaching Secular Peoples: A Review of the Books of George G. Hunter, III." *The Asbury Journal* 66, no. 2 (2011): 108-119. https://place.asburyseminary.edu/cgi/viewcontent.cgi?referer=https://www.google.com/&httpsredir=1&article=1140&context=asburyjournal (5 February

2021).

McRae, Mary B., Patricia M. Carey, and Roxanna Anderson-Scott. "Black Churches as Therapeutic Systems: A Group Process Perspective." *Health Education & Behavior* 25, no. 6 (1998): 778-789.

Shareefa, Mariyam, Rohani Hj Awg Mat Zin, Nor Zaiham Midawati Abdullah, and Rosmawijah Jawawi. "Differentiated Instruction: Definition and Challenging Factors Perceived by Teachers." *Proceedings of the 3rd International Conference on Special Education (ICSE 2019)* 388 (2019): 322-327. https://www.atlantis-press.com/proceedings/icse-19/125928885 (5 February 2021).

Van Der Stuyf, Rachel R. "Scaffolding as a Teaching Strategy." *Adolescent Learning and Development* 52, no. 3 (2002): 1-13. http://ateachingpath1.weebly.com/uploads/1/7/8/9/17892507/stuyf_2002.pdf (5 January 2021).

Whitney, William B., and Pamela Ebstyne King. "Religious Congregations and Communities." In *Emerging Adults' Religiousness and Spirituality: Meaning- Making in an Age of Transition*, ed. Carolyn McNamara Barry and Mona M. Abo- Zena, 133-151. New York: Oxford University Press, 2014.

Williams, Morgan K. "John Dewey in the 21st Century." *Journal of Inquiry and Action in Education* 9, no. 1 (2017): 91-102. https://digitalcommons.buffalostate.edu/cgi/viewcontent.cgi?article=1147&context=jiae (5 February 2021).

Other Sources

Bible Study Tools. "Greek Lexicon Entry for *Ekklesia*." *The KJV New Testament Greek Lexicon*. On *Biblestudytools.com*. N.d. https://www.biblestudytools.com/lexicons/greek/kjv/ekklesia.html (3 July 2020).

Cherry, Kendra. "History and Key Concepts of Behavioral Psychology." *Verywellmind.com*. 20 February 2021. http://psychology.about.com/od/behavioralpsychology/f/behaviorism.htm (15 March 2021).

Cru. "Step 13: Establish Discipleship Relationships." *Cru.org*. N.d. https://www.cru.org/car/en/train-and-grow/leadership-training/starting-a-ministry/growing/step-13-establish-discipleship-relationships.html (12 October 2019).

Hagedorn, Linda Serra. "How to Define Retention: A New Look at an Old Problem." *Eric.ed.gov*. 2006. https://files.eric.ed.gov/fulltext/ED493674.pdf (5 February 2021).

Herrick, Greg. "2. Understanding the Meaning of the Term 'Disciple.'" *Bible.org*. 11 May 2004. https://bible.org/seriespage/2-understanding-meaning-term-disciple (20 March 2021).

Huitt, W., and J. Hummel. "Piaget's Theory of Cognitive Development." *Edpsycinteractive.org*. 2003. http://www.edpsycinteractive.org/topics/cognition/

piaget.html (5 February 2021).

Jei, In Ho. "A Strategy on Small Group Leadership Development for Transitioning of Gaeumjung Church into a Cell-Based Church." D.Min. proj., Liberty Theological Seminary, 2008.

Kahn Academy. "Classical and Operant Conditioning Article." *Khanacademy.org*. N.d. https://www.khanacademy.org/test-prep/mcat/behavior/learning-slug/a/classical- and-operant-conditioning-article (5 February 2021).

Kim, Ho Kyung. "The Biblical Approach to Church Growth through Personal Evangelism." D.Min. proj., Liberty Baptist Theological Seminary, 2000.

Kuh, George D., and Ken O'Donnell. "Figure 2: High-Impact Practices: Eight Key Elements and Examples." *Ts3.nashonline.org*. 2013. http://ts3.nashonline.org/wp-content/uploads/2018/04/AACU-LEAP-High-Impact-Practice-Characteristics.pdf (5 February 2021).

Lundgren, Martha. "A Plan for Congregational and Pastoral Care Giving with Our Senior and Elder Members." *Umcstmarks.org*. April 2016. https://pdf4pro.com/amp/view/a-plan-for-congregational-and-pastoral-care-giving-238a72.html (5 February 2021).

Machel, Edgar. "The Relationship Between Leadership Traits and Church Growth Among Pastors of Free Churches in Germany." Ph.D. diss., Andrews University, 2006. https://digitalcommons.andrews.edu/cgi/viewcontent.cgi?article=1545&

context=dissertations (5 February 2021).

Morrison, Michael. "Acts 1:15-26—Another Apostle is Chosen." *Gcs.edu*. 2012. https://learn.gcs.edu/mod/book/view.php?id=4475&chapterid=50 (5 February 2021).

Russ, Eric. "Fellowship." *Discipleshipdefined.com*. 2013. http://www. discipleshipdefined.com/resources/fellowship (5 February 2021).

Saddleback Church. "Our Church." *Saddleback.com*. N.d. https://saddleback.com/visit/ about/our-church (5 January 2021).

_____. "Our Pastor." *Saddleback.com*. N.d. https://saddleback.com/visit/about/pastors/our-pastor (5 January 2021).

Seamands, John. "What McGavran's Church Growth Thesis Means." *Missionexus.org*. 1 October 1966. https://missionexus.org/what-mcgavrans-church-growth-thesis-means/ (5 February 2021).

Send Institute., "Church Planting Manifesto." *Sendinstitute.org*. N.d. https:// www.sendinstitute.org/wp-content/uploads/2019/02/2.7-Draft-Send-Institute- Church-Planting-Manifesto-for-North-America.pdf (11 December 2020).

University of Houston. "About Constructivism." *Uh.edu*. N.d. https://uh.edu/charter- school/about-us/about-constructivism/ (5 February 2021).

University of Wisconsin Eau Claire. "High-Impact

Small Groups: A Discipleship Model | 257

Practices." *Uwec.edu*. N.d. https://www.uwec.edu/acadaff/academic-master-plan/high-impact-practices/#:~:text= High%2Dimpact%20practices%2C%20or%20HIPs,on%20 Student%20 Engagement%20(NSSE) (30 April 2021).

Verenikina, I. "Scaffolding and Learning: Its Role in Nurturing New Learners." *Ro.uow. edu.au*. May 2008. https://ro.uow.edu.au/cgi/viewcontent.cgi?article=1043& context=edupapers (5 February 2021).

Warren, Rick. "Twelve Characteristics of a Purpose Driven Church." *Pd.church*. N.d. https://pd.church/12-characteristics-purpose-driven-church/ (12 January 2021).

_____. "Small Groups: 4 Kinds that Expand Ministry." *Pastors.com*. 1 October 2012. https://pastors.com/small-groups-4-kinds-that-expand-ministry/ (6 February 2021).

Whitney, Donald S. "Cultivate Koinonia." *Biblicalspirituality.org*. 2002. https://biblicalspirituality.org/wp-content/uploads/2011/01/Cultivate-Koinonia.pdf (5 February 2021).

TABLES

1. Ages — 164
2. Genders — 166
3. Ethnicities — 169
4. Employment — 172
5. Marital Status — 174
6. Education — 177
7. Number of Small Groups Attended that Emphasized Any Topic of Biblical Teaching, Education, Life Skills, or Personal Development — 180
8. Small Group Experience Addresses the Need for Accountability — 187
9. Small Group Experience Addresses the Need for Fellowship — 190
10. Small Group Experience Addresses the Need for Leadership Development — 193
11. Small Group Experience Addresses the Need for Charity/Service Work — 196
12. Small Group Experience Addresses the Need for Church Member Care and Engagement — 199
13. Small Group Experience Addresses the Need for Organization by Leader — 201
14. Small Group Experience Addresses the Need for Message Dissemination — 203
15. Small Group Experience Addresses the — 206

Need for Impartation of Spiritual Gifts	
16. Small Group Experience Addresses the Need for Increase of Church Attendance	209
17. Small Group Experience Addresses the Need for Intercessory Work	212
18. Able to Access Small Groups Supplementary Resources at My Church	215
19. Increase of Tithes and Offerings Since Implementing Small Groups	217
20. Increase in Church Attendance Since Implementing Small Groups	220
21. Increase of Volunteer Population Since Implementing Small Groups	222
22. Increase in Fellowship Attendance Since Implementing Small Groups	225
23. Increase in Altar Calls Since Implementing Small Groups	228
24. Increase in Small Group Attendance Since Implementing Small Groups	231
25. Increase of Small Group Leaders Since Implementing Small Groups	233
26. Increase of Baptism Participants Since Implementing Small Groups	235

Larry Lawrence Brandon, Jr., DMin

Biography

Psalm 37:23 says, "The steps of a good man are ordered by the Lord..." This scripture perfectly encapsulates the life and ministry of Bishop Larry Lawrence Brandon, a devoted servant of God and humanity. As the Founder of Praise Temple, one of the most vibrant congregations in the Shreveport-Bossier City area, Bishop Brandon has spent decades building a ministry that is dynamic, impactful, and community-focused. He also serves as the Third Presiding Bishop of the Full Gospel Baptist Church Fellowship International, founded by his pastor, Bishop Paul S. Morton, Sr., and now led by Bishop J. Warren Walker. His leadership extends beyond the pulpit, having served as the Chairman of the Tehillah Music Group and contributed to many other initiatives within the Fellowship. His influence as a minister, mentor, counselor, speaker, radio personality, and spiritual father has shaped countless lives. Additionally, he founded L.L. Brandon Ministries, Inc., through which he consults for nonprofits and small businesses, helping them thrive and expand their community impact.

In 2022, Bishop Brandon was presented as the third pastor of the historic Evergreen Missionary Baptist Church in Oakland, California. His visionary leadership and Spirit-led teachings have inspired, instructed, and transformed lives, leading the congregation and the community into a new season of growth and spiritual renewal.

A United States Air Force Veteran, Bishop Brandon's dedication to service reaches beyond the church. His leadership in the community includes serving as a Life Member of the historic Alpha Phi Alpha Fraternity, Inc., 100

Black Men of the Bay area, former Chairman of the Shreveport Regional Airport Authority Board, from which he stepped down to accept an appointment to the Louisiana State Ethics Board, elected by the Louisiana House of Representatives. His chaplaincy work spans several key institutions, including the Louisiana State Police, Public Safety Services, Caddo Parish District Attorney's Office, Bossier Parish District Attorney's Office, Shreveport Fire Department, and the Shreveport City Marshal's Office.

Bishop Brandon was honored with an invitation to serve as Guest Chaplain for the United States House of Representatives in Washington, D.C., at the request of the 56th House Speaker, the Honorable James Michael Johnson. Also, he was inducted into an elite group of religious leaders and awarded the Honorary Guest Chaplain Pin for his service to the House of Representatives. Moreover, Bishop Brandon received the distinguished invitation to serve as Guest Chaplain for the United States Senate, extended by Louisiana Senator Bill Cassidy, further recognizing his commitment to faith and public service at the highest levels of government.

Bishop Brandon is actively involved in civic engagement as a co-founder and Former Board Member of the Step Forward Children's Education Initiative, Adult Prisoner's Reentry Initiative, and the Rotary Club of Shreveport. His extensive board memberships and commissions reflect his commitment to service. He is the Managing Partner of Brandon Group International LLC, he leads as the Facility Administrator and Center Director of the L.L. Brandon III Transitional Home for Boys, and the Chief Executive Officer and Executive Director of the Northwest Louisiana Community Development Corporation. Bishop Brandon also serves as the President/CEO of Evergreen Terrace Housing Corporation, Evergreen Annexed, Inc., President of the Evergreen Community Development Corporation.

In 2000, he completed his Episcopal Studies and Continuing Education at the prestigious Joint College of African American Bishops in Vatican City, Rome, Italy, and completed the Summer Leader Program at Harvard Divinity. In 2005, Bishop Larry Brandon served as Chancellor of the University Christian Preparatory School in Shreveport, Louisiana, overseeing educational programs for students from Pre-K3 through 12th grade and a Certified Adverse Childhood Experience (ACE) Educator. His commitment to education culminated in earning his Doctorate of Ministry in Church Ministries and Leadership from Oral Roberts University.

In addition to his pastoral duties, Bishop Brandon is a prolific author. His groundbreaking books include From Private Pain to Public Victory, Treasures in the Darkness, Holiness Is Still Right, A Faith That Feels Like Lying, and You Complete Me, a profound exploration of cultivating a godly marriage, co-authored with his wife, Wanda L. Brandon.

A beloved pastor, teacher, mentor, and father, Bishop Brandon is deeply committed to his family and community. He is the proud father of five children: Queenesia, Jasmine, Isaiah, Elijah, and the late Larry III. His prayer for every individual he encounters is that they be blessed, challenged, inspired, and transformed. His guiding motto is simple yet powerful: "We are better together."

www.ingramcontent.com/pod-product-compliance
Lightning Source LLC
Chambersburg PA
CBHW060817190426
43197CB00038B/1839